A FREE FLAME

Ann-Marie Priest grew up in country South Australia, but has lived most of her adult life in rural Queensland. She writes essays and reviews, and her first book, *Great Writers, Great Loves: The Reinvention of Love in the Twentieth-Century*, explored the love lives of a group of influential twentieth-century writers. She has a PhD in English literature and teaches at Central Queensland University.

A FREE FLAME
Australian Women Writers and Vocation in the Twentieth Century

Ann-Marie Priest

UWA PUBLISHING

First published in 2018 by
UWA Publishing
Crawley, Western Australia 6009
www.uwap.uwa.edu.au

UWAP is an imprint of UWA Publishing
a division of The University of Western Australia

THE UNIVERSITY OF
WESTERN
AUSTRALIA

A catalogue record for this
book is available from the
National Library of Australia

Permission to reproduce the work of Ruth Park courtesy of the copyright owners, Kemalde Pty Ltd c/- Tim Curnow Literary Agent and Consultant, Sydney.

Parts of Chapter 1 appeared in the journal *Hecate* (vol. 40, no. 2, 2014) as 'Baby and Demon: Woman and the Artist in the Poetry of Gwen Harwood'.

Cover design by Peter Long
Typeset in Bembo by Lasertype
Printed by McPherson's Printing Group

This project is supported by the Copyright Agency Cultural Fund.

This project has been assisted by the Australian Government through the Australia Council for the Arts, its arts funding and advisory body.

 uwapublishing

The poet's vocation — or, more precisely, the historical
construction put upon it — is one of the single, most
problematic areas for any woman who comes to the craft.
Not only has it been defined by a tradition which could
never foresee her, but it is construed by men about men,
in ways which are poignant, compelling and exclusive.

Eavan Boland, *Object Lessons*

For it's not only a room of her own and an income that
a woman needs — though that is often hard enough
to come by — but the place in herself, the space in her
soul from which she can withstand the onslaught of a
world that cannot, or will not, take her seriously.

Drusilla Modjeska, *Stravinsky's Lunch*

This is a love that equals in its power the love of
man for woman and reaches inwards as deeply.
It is the love of a man or of a woman for their
world. For the world of their centre where their
lives burn genuinely and with a free flame.

Mervyn Peake, *Titus Groan*

Contents

Introduction

For writers, painters and performers of all stripes to talk about a sense of calling is commonplace these days. The idea that art is destiny, that the artist has no choice but to follow their vocation, has become a well-established part of popular discourse. For this very reason, perhaps, the concept of the artist's vocation is easy to dismiss. It has been invoked too often, and in too many situations where it simply does not apply. As well, its romance has been used to disguise unacknowledged privilege, depicting an individual artist's success as entirely the result of their own personal qualities and glossing over the social and cultural advantages that readied the platform for them.

Nevertheless, the concept has played an important role in the way artists, and particularly writers, have understood themselves and their lives over the past century and more, and as such it warrants a closer look. Many writers speak in powerful terms of a sense of being born to write, of feeling compelled to return again and again to their art, of being driven to become a writer against all obstacles. Their sense that their profession is at the heart of their identity goes well beyond the narratives that generally surround concepts like 'ambition' and 'career'. Even in contexts that are profoundly secular, their words evoke the religious origins of the notion of vocation as the life to which one is called by God.

Precisely why this concept is so important to writers, why so many turn to it again and again, what it means to them and what role it plays in their construction of their identities as writers are questions worth exploring – most especially in relation to women writers. If a writer's sense of vocation in general often seems unaccountable, it is more mysterious still for writers who are female, since until the last century almost all models of the literary artist were male. How does a woman come to believe that she is called to a profession – more, an identity – that specifically excludes her? Many cultural critics, from Virginia Woolf in the 1920s to Eavan Boland, Elaine Showalter, Ellen Moers and Carolyn Heilbrun at the end of the century to, most recently, Drusilla Modjeska, Carolyn Korsmeyer and Toril Moi, have pointed out the ways in which the Western ideal of the artist is in direct opposition to the Western ideal of woman. The artist speaks, while the woman is silent; the artist is active and ambitious, while the woman is passive and self-abnegating; the artist's highest calling is art, while the woman's is motherhood; the artist drinks deeply from the well of experience, while the woman is chaste, her life circumscribed. As these critics and others have pointed out, such conventions have meant that women have had to violate some powerful norms of female behaviour and, indeed, female identity, in order to create for themselves an identity as an artist. Because such conventions have been internalised as well as enforced and reinforced externally by their culture, this has sometimes led women writers into complicated psychological and social contortions that have been deeply destructive for them.

The concept of vocation, however, has the power to cut across such constraints. Vocation is an invitation into the space of the artist's identity, an unequivocal authorisation of the aspirant's ambitions. The person with a literary vocation asserts that, far from choosing a particular career path out of interest or ambition, she has been hailed into her role, even against her own will. She has been chosen, by forces too mysterious to be challenged, and this in itself is proof that she has a right to be an artist, that even as a woman she can have an artist's identity. In the early part of the twentieth century, when there was so little evidence that a woman could fill this role and so much hostility towards any attempt by a woman to do so, this was an extraordinarily transgressive thing to claim.

The aim of this book is to explore the ways in which four Australian writers – Tasmanian poet and librettist Gwen Harwood, West Australian poet, playwright and novelist Dorothy Hewett, expatriate novelist Christina Stead, and Sydney journalist, children's writer and novelist Ruth Park – came to claim a sense of vocation, and the significance of this claim for their lives, identities and careers. My focus is on the stories they told about themselves as writers, whether overtly autobiographical or fictionalised. Thus I have drawn on their autobiographical writings, where they exist, including both published and unpublished letters, as well as on key poems, plays and novels. My aim is to tease out their narratives of vocation in order to establish a sense of how they were able to authorise themselves to become artists at a time when 'woman' and 'artist' were generally considered to be mutually exclusive terms.

Along the way, I look at the costs for these writers of aspiring to an identity so much at odds with their cultural identity as women. Deep tensions and anxieties are evident in their stories, which sometimes threaten to derail their vocation narratives, but which also help to illuminate the risks for women of claiming an artist's identity. For Harwood, the pressure points emerge around the old bugbear of selfishness, her fear that to give free rein to the artist within would turn her from devoted wife and mother to unconscionable monster. For Hewett, the fear was that the artist's need for solitude and single-minded devotion to her work would cut her off from the adventurer's life of love and passion that was itself the lifeblood of her art. For Stead, assuming an artist's identity was accompanied by a pervasive fear that she would be judged unacceptable as a woman, and open to the scorn and derision meted out to the 'old maids' of her youth. For Park, the tension was between the idealised freedom of the artist to find her own voice and the commercial imperatives that constrain a busy professional woman with a family to support.

In these women's stories, there are no easy resolutions. All four struggled throughout their lives to make a place for themselves — as women, wives, mothers and lovers, as people bound in complex ways to others and to their communities — within the discourse of art and artists. But their struggles show both the power and the malleability of social and cultural ideals in the ongoing exchange within each life between the individual and their world. Vocation is one of the key points of intersection between the personal and the social, between what individuals feel within themselves and how they operate in the world. These women's stories show them using this point of intersection to change their lives. In the process, they also change the concepts of both woman and artist so that these two opposing ideals may begin to encompass one another.

Demon Lover

Gwen Harwood

Gwen Harwood's most direct account of the development of her writing ambitions appears in *Blessed City*, a selection of letters she wrote in wartime Brisbane when she was in her early twenties to Tony Riddell, a new friend on active service in the navy. At the time, she was not a poet – far from it. She was working in the War Damage Commission, a public service institution set up to provide insurance against possible damage resulting from World War II. She found the organisation ludicrous in every aspect, from its aims to its processes to its earnest employees, and in a spirit half of mischief, half of outrage, she began a one-person campaign of mocking, corrupting and destabilising it. Her behaviour was extraordinary. She developed an impenetrable filing system, explicable to no one but herself. She inserted made-up people into the official records. She dedicated long hours at her desk to cutting out cardboard animals and writing private letters. She even staged elaborate phone conversations in German with imaginary interlocutors. Many years later she would tell a friend that she could not imagine how she was not fired, or at least moved on.[1]

Her reports on her antics are hilarious, but along with the spirit of sheer anarchy that runs through her letters, there is also a vein of outraged incredulity. It is as though she can hardly believe that such things as bureaucracies exist, and, worse, that sensible people can be expected to devote precious years of their lives to ensuring their smooth functioning. Beneath her gleeful exposure of her boss's stupidity or the office manager's mindless conformity is a wild rebellion over the nature of work. When her boss, whom she calls Mafeking, declares to his secretary that he is 'in love' with his work, she almost explodes: 'Work! The work he does could not be taken seriously by any person whose brain was normally developed.'[2] Elsewhere, she says that she finds the place almost intolerably depressing: 'Sometimes the thought of the time I'm wasting against my will and the minds, sluggish and infected, of the people round me all day, fills me with heaviness which I cannot shake off.'[3]

Her job at the War Damage Commission was very far from the life she had envisaged for herself as a child. Throughout *Blessed City*, beneath the high spirits and ferocious wit, is the sense that she herself is lost. 'I am unsettled and restless because I haven't really found what I should be doing with my life', she tells Riddell. 'I feel that I am corked up in a bottle, and this is because I'm not really doing what I should be doing, whatever it may be.'[4] That 'whatever it may be' sounds as though she really does not know what she wants to do. But it is easy to see from the letters alone that she had a strong sense of vocation. She was writing poems, plays and stories in her spare time, and showing them to Riddell and other friends whose opinion she respected. She even sent some poems to the newly founded literary magazine *Meanjin*. She was also studying piano and organ at a high level, and learning composition. Yet she did not say to Riddell that she wanted to be an artist. In fact, when he asked her outright if she could see herself as a writer, she said no. 'If I decided to be a writer I should certainly long to be something else in about three months, so it seems better to do nothing at all about it', she explained.[5] A little later, she airily declared that she was not worried about her vocation because if all else failed, she could always write.

This blithe denial of any ambition in relation to what would become her life's work may have arisen from the disappointment she had recently suffered over her first attempt to become an artist. As a child, Harwood had had a very robust sense of vocation: she wanted to be a concert pianist, and received every encouragement in this, not only from her ambitious mother but also from her teachers and friends. She earned her AMusA (Associate in Music Australia) before she left school, and seems to have been something of a star pupil, performing at a concert at Brisbane Town Hall at 16, and a year later being taken by her teacher to play for

Arthur Rubinstein, then a towering musical figure, during his visit to Brisbane. A review in the *Courier Mail* of the 1936 concert singles out the 16-year-old Gwen Foster from the other student performers for her 'impressive accomplishment', declaring that 'this pianist already has brilliance in her technical handling of exacting passages, and with it something without which technique may go for little'.[6] This 'something' the critic dubs 'an innate music-consciousness', before going on to conclude that the young woman 'has a future at the piano'. The newspaper's report of Harwood's 'audition' with Rubinstein is similarly laudatory: 'Mr. Rubinstein told Miss Foster he was impressed by her technique and her artistic sensibilities and considered it would be well worth her while to study abroad.'[7] In 1939, at the age of 19, she qualified for her ATCL (Associate Diploma Trinity College, London) and was awarded a Silver Medal, tying with another student for the highest marks in the Trinity College examinations.[8] But by this time she had already given up her dream of becoming a professional musician.

The existing biographical sources – chiefly Harwood's letters and interviews, and Gregory Kratzmann's introductory matter for his volume of her selected correspondence – are ambiguous about exactly how this came about. When Harwood left school at 17, she intended to devote herself to music, and began to study both performance and composition with a new teacher, Dr Robert Dalley-Scarlett. She also began to learn the organ, work as an accompanist and transcriber, and sing with the Brisbane Handel Society, as well as taking on a few pupils of her own. But she soon stopped thinking that she would become a concert pianist. In an essay, she says that it was Dalley-Scarlett who broke the news to her that she was not good enough to have a concert career. 'The good musical Doctor told me firmly that I would never make it as a concert pianist', she writes.[9] She elaborates further in an interview, in which she explains that 'I wasn't as good as I thought':

> I hadn't at that time really understood how a good pianist should be out and clear by the time they're about 15. I was adequate, I was a good accompanist, I'd developed quite a good skill as a sight-reader...[10]

Here, she tails off. We are left to infer that for all her ability, she was no musical genius.

She adds that she had her first intimation that 'something was missing' when she played for Rubinstein at the Bellevue Hotel. Her previous music teacher, Hardy Gerhardy, had taken her there one evening, still in her school uniform, and talked Rubinstein into hearing her play. Halfway through her performance, she glanced around to see how he was taking it. 'I saw out of the corner of my eye Rubinstein yawning', she says, 'and he was yawning monumentally'. Her failure to hold the great man's attention struck her as a bad sign. Many years later, she would make this moment the pivot on which a woman's life turns in the poem 'Suburban Sonnet': because Rubinstein yawned, the poem seems to say, a promising young pianist became a downtrodden housewife, distracted by her children, desperately trying to make something meaningful out of the recycled scraps of her life. Harwood's own experience was not quite like that, however; she did not walk out of the Bellevue Hotel and immediately abandon all her musical aspirations. Just the opposite, in fact: it was soon after this that she left school to take up full-time music study. But the experience was emblematic, in her mind: it stood for her failure to make the grade as an artist.

To her readers, however, the incident may be emblematic of something quite different: the power of men in a patriarchal society to pass judgement on women's creativity. At that time, it is fair to say, there was not much interest in women as artists; indeed, there was still doubt that women were capable of high levels of achievement in any field. The much-respected Edwardian novelist Arnold Bennett wrote in 1920 that 'No woman at all has achieved…music that is better than second-rate', and this view seems to have reflected the dominant consensus.[11] Harwood herself would say many years later that it was not until the 'age of recording' – well into the twentieth century – that it could at last be seen that 'some of the really great pianists are women'.[12] The young Harwood was trying to build a musical career for herself at a time when women were more likely to be seen by established musicians as potential conquests or playthings than as colleagues and future collaborators[13], and Harwood's experience as a music student seems to reflect this.

A handful of loosely autobiographical poems she wrote about this period are revealing. The poem 'A Simple Story', for instance, is based on her real-life meeting with conductor Percy Code. It describes how at 17 a young musician goes to see a 'visiting conductor' in his hotel room to show him her composition. He turns out to be far more interested in her body than her music, putting 'one hand on the manuscript / and the other down [her] dress', and dismissing her score with a patronising 'That's *lovely*, dear'. From this, she deduces 'that I was no composer'. In a letter written some 20 years after the incident, she gives a spoof version of events, saying that she met the 'conductor of the X orchestra' one afternoon and showed him her 'unaccompanied motet': 'Felt a pang of tenderness as he tried to seduce me on the shadow-barred grass by the golden-coated river.'[14] She does not elaborate on the fate of her motet, but it seems likely she drew the same conclusion about her composing talent as the young woman in her poem.

Her poem 'David's Harp' is similarly based on an actual incident in her life, an encounter (one of many) with a Scottish tenor named Will who, like Harwood, sang with the Handel Society. In a letter, Harwood describes him, with affection, as 'a notorious philanderer' with a 'plain, nice, Scottish wife and two or possibly more plain, nice Scottish children'.[15] In the poem, a 17-year-old girl (once again) is practising on a church organ one Saturday morning when a tenor comes in, an older man ('He must be thirty, if a day'). She plays and he sings, making his way through the church to the organ until he stands beside her. He

> puts his arms around
> my waist and squeezes me until
> I gasp, then gently lifts my hands
> to his, and kisses me.

Like the visiting conductor before him, the tenor clearly has no interest in the girl's musicianship. In fact, his definitive act is to take her hands from the keyboard – stopping her from playing – in order to embrace her.

Harwood herself did not resent such behaviour – far from it. When she writes about these two incidents in letters, she describes them in highly playful and comic terms, and pities the men for the chase she led them. She does note that she was 'a natural target in those far-off days for musicians'[16], but does not seem offended that these men, and others like them, who had the power to authorise her musical ambitions, chose instead to treat her as a plaything. Nor does she wonder whether she might have felt differently about her artistic abilities if such men had taken her seriously as a composer or musician, and welcomed her as a kind of apprentice into their fraternity. While her confidence in herself as a sexual being was boosted by their attentions, her confidence as an artist was undermined. Perhaps this was one reason she was initially reluctant to own her new vocation as a poet in her letters to Riddell. She may well have felt that the men she knew would be no more likely to take her writing ambitions seriously than they had her musical ones. In any case, she seems to have made no real attempts to establish a writing career at this early stage. Instead, at 25, after several years of drifting, she married Bill Harwood and moved with him to Tasmania, where she quite quickly had four children. She gave up the piano – she had no instrument to play – and she stopped writing. She would later say that she 'immured' herself[17], an idea that is echoed in a number of her poems about this time in her life, in which she uses images of being entombed, imprisoned, walled up. In her own terms, she buried her gift.

With her marriage, Harwood would later write, her 'life as a practising musician came to an end'.[18] It seems to be no coincidence that at the same time, she encountered 'an anguish I had never known'.[19] One of her early poems begins: 'Hands, nerves know this. I mourn for my lost skill.'[20] It is a sentiment she would express in letters over many years, speaking of how 'The absence of music from my fingertips is sometimes unbearable; "nothing can equal it in depth of pain"'.[21]

But her sense of grief went beyond this specific loss. It was one thing to let go of her music, but another thing entirely to let go of her sense of herself as an artist. In letters to Riddell written after she married, she several times suggests a connection between giving up music and taking up poetry. The loss of music, she says in one letter, was a kind of wound from which poetry helped her to heal: 'I was driven to seek wholeness and forced to develop in another way, as a blind man in his eternal night must sharpen his other senses.'[22] Only through art, she seems to say, could she be whole; the particular form she chose, music or poetry, was not important. The same idea crops up in an earlier letter to Riddell in which, smarting over rejections of her poems, she toys with giving up poetry and returning to music, as though the two are entirely interchangeable. 'If only I had kept my musical skill I could leave poetry (a rat leaving a sinking ship?) and settle down to Mozart and Haydn', she writes.[23] It seems clear that in her mind, she must have some form of artistic work, whether music or poetry. Giving up poetry with no alternative artistic practice to replace it with was simply not conceivable.

This may be why, as a young mother, she fought so hard to keep open a space in her crowded days for poetry. The realities of her marriage seem to have come as something of a shock to her. She married in great love and was eager to have children and to enter fully into her new life. But suddenly – or so it seemed – she found that she no longer knew herself. She had been transformed into somebody else, with all the things that had once been so important to her – music, poetry, friends, her own independent, questing existence – utterly banished. One of the keys to this state of mind is her poem 'Lip Service', which she wrote in the late 1950s or early 1960s but which remained unpublished during her lifetime. In this poem, a woman speaks of her determination to subdue her desire to write and instead devote herself entirely to being a housewife and mother. She describes this self-subdual as the process of 'coring' herself like a piece of fruit – of cutting out her own heart. Once purged of the 'seeds' of restlessness, bitterness and grief, she will be free to

> serve the mild
> Fruit of myself to fill the needs
> Of husband and importuning child.

As for her buried yearning, she will simply shut her ears to its cries:

> And when I hear the parable
> Of the talents preached, I'll say 'My one
> Talent is to keep house. Heart shall
> Not beat in vain like a winged stone.'

But when, after making this bitter sacrifice, she looks at herself in the mirror, she does not recognise the 'sad face' staring back at her 'with an idiot grin'. In her desire for a calm and painless acceptance of her lot, she has sacrificed the part of her that makes her who she is.

Harwood's letters from that time show her own frustration at having so little time to write, as well as her occasional wish to put aside her troublesome literary ambitions. There is a part of her that wants to be nothing more than a devoted wife and mother, surrendering herself uncomplainingly, like the woman in her poem, to her husband and children for their nourishment and sustenance. Yet she cannot let go of her writing ambitions, any more than her fictional alter ego can. Like the woman in her poem, Harwood believes she has an obligation not to shut her ears to the Parable of the Talents, a story told by Jesus in the New Testament to illustrate the idea that each person has a divinely imposed obligation to make the most of the abilities they were born with. By denying her gift for writing and asserting that her only talent is 'to keep house', the woman in Harwood's poem sins against this sacred imperative. The consequences, as the poem makes clear, are severe: because she buries her God-given gifts, she is alienated from herself and abandoned by God. The final line of the poem is a Biblical shunning: 'Then what have I to do with thee?' These are the words Jesus uses to rebuke his mother in another gospel story (John 2:4), as well as those spoken to Jesus by an 'unclean spirit' to mark its distance from the holy (Mark 5:7). Harwood herself was not prepared to risk such a fate. Though she increasingly felt that her 'gift', as she called it, was 'hateful' to her, she could not turn her back on it. To do so would be to risk destruction.

The Parable of the Talents was central to the way Harwood came to think of her vocation. In a much later poem, she would evoke the story again when reminiscing about conversations she had held with friends in her youth on the subject of 'how not to put aside / that talent which is death to hide'.[24] The lines echo the famous poem by John Milton, 'On His Blindness', which Harwood would certainly have known. In this poem, Milton laments his encroaching loss of vision, fearing that if he loses his sight, he will be unable to continue to write poetry. The idea of 'that one talent which is death to hide / Lodg'd with me useless' fills him with despair. To hide his 'talent' – that is, his God-given gift for poetry – is to court death. He knows that, like the unworthy servant in the parable who buried his 'talent' instead of investing it, he will face a reckoning for such wastage.

The idea that God requires us to make use of the gifts he has given us proved to be a surprisingly powerful one for women writers in the nineteenth century. In Charlotte Brontë's novel *Shirley*, for instance, 12-year-old Rose Yorke uses the Parable of the Talents to insist that she has a duty to 'trade' with her God-given talents, rather than 'bury' them in household chores. In the US around the same time, women writers took heart from Transcendentalist philosophies that told them they were beholden 'only to God' in working out their 'higher calling'.[25] Almost a century later, Virginia Woolf would secularise the concept in *A Room of One's Own*, speaking of the 'poison of fear and bitterness' bred in women who could not pursue their own deepest desires but instead were forced to dedicate themselves to uncongenial work in order to support themselves.[26] Using herself as an example, she writes that on top of the drudgery and poor pay the female worker experiences, she is oppressed by the loss of her own unique talent:

the thought of that one gift which it was death to hide – a small one but dear to the possessor – perishing

and with it my self, my soul – all this became like a
rust eating away the bloom of the spring, destroying
the tree at its heart.

For Woolf, as for Milton, the 'gift which it was death to
hide' is the desire to write. But the 'death' Woolf fears
is not eternal damnation, as it was for Milton. Instead, it
is a kind of psychic extinction: the loss of 'my self, my
soul'. The woman who does not fulfil her vocation risks
a kind of metaphorical damnation, the loss of the very
core of the self.

Harwood understood the metaphor of the 'gift that is
death to hide' in very much the same way. She had given
up her Anglican faith around the time of her marriage,
but she nevertheless saw this parable as expressing a
binding truth. The very existence of her poetic 'gift'
carried with it the obligation to develop it; she could
not abandon her vocation, no matter how inconvenient
it was, or how much easier it would have been to give it
up, because it was a sacred responsibility. If it was painful
to acknowledge, it was even more painful to ignore or
repress. Nevertheless, there were times when she seemed
to consider doing exactly that. 'Sometimes it is agony for
me to be in labour with a poem', she wrote to a friend
in 1961. 'I must speak the truth & the truth is terrible'.[27]
She added that at such times, she wished herself 'rid of
the gift that tears me apart'.

The reason for this seems to be largely the one she sets
out in 'Lip Service': the unresolvable conflict between
the requirements of her role as wife and mother and

those of her life as an artist. In letters written in her early thirties, she tells of feeling 'oppressed by the endless routine tasks one has caring for very young children', of the frustration of being forced to snatch her 'private life in ten-minute stretches', and of her longing for 'peace and solitude'.[28] Many years later, she would write of the early years of her marriage: 'If I had the time again I should be much fiercer, and DEMAND time for myself'.[29] In interviews, she often speaks of how she would prop books up over the sink to read while she was doing the dishes – 'they'd get puffy with soap splashes'.[30] This speaks volumes about her determination to hold on to this vanishing part of her life. And then there is 'An Impromptu for Ann Jennings', in which she speaks of her feeling, during the years of 'cleaning up infants and the floors they muddied', that her spirit was in bondage and crying for release, expression, embodiment: 'spirit beat at flesh as in a grave // from which it could not rise'.

Yet despite her frustration, and even her fury, during these years, Harwood made no real attempt to 'DEMAND time' for herself. To do so, she believed, would have been heartless – a violation of her identity as a woman. Her letters show the degree to which, in her mind, the poet and the woman were antagonistic identities. 'Rilke fed his genius at the expense of everything else', she wrote to Riddell in 1960 of the great German poet. 'He would have scorned utterly my attempts to combine domesticity with poetry'.[31] Such attempts, she went on, were themselves proof of a fatal softness towards others – fatal to poetry, that is: 'I think that real genius brings with it the necessary hardness; I haven't got the final streak of hardness, and lack the corresponding stratum of talent'. To be a 'true' poet, her letters often suggest, she would need to turn her back on the needs of her children and her husband, and this she was not prepared to do.

Her sense that to focus on her poetry instead of her children would be monstrous is given expression in 'Burning Sappho'. In this poem, a woman tries all day to find a few moments to write but is thwarted at every turn by the demands of her child, friends and household. Each time, a murderous 'fiend' or 'monster' rises up in her and is quelled. When, in the quiet evening, she finally sits down with her pen, she is compelled yet again to meet someone else's needs: 'My husband calls me, rich in peace, to bed'. Though she smilingly complies, she is boiling with rage: 'In my warm thighs a fleshless devil / chops him to bits with hell-cold evil.' This 'fleshless devil' is the close kin of the earlier fiend, who had sought to perform voodoo on her toddler and pour 'prussic acid' on the visiting rector. Yet he is also justified, in the terms of the poem, which cries out in its very form and structure that this woman, this unsung Sappho, has a right to be a poet, and that those who fail to recognise this right deserve their fate.

Nevertheless, the demon, though evoked, is not unleashed. Burning Sappho does not go on the rampage and destroy those she has bound herself to protect in order to carve out some time for herself. Instead, she swallows her impatience, does what she is required to do, and waits it out, finally snatching some time to write from sleep. Harwood's letters suggest that this was her strategy, too. As angry as she often felt at being so completely at the service of the needs and desires of others, and as convinced as she was that her calling to be a poet deserved to be respected, she was not prepared to become a monster – which was how she saw the woman who turned her back on her roles as housewife and mother in order to serve the Muse. Further, she felt the need – intermittently, at least – to hide her anger. 'One of my troubles is recurrent respectability', she told her friend Edwin Tanner in a 1962 letter. 'I have fits of it (unpredictable) and wish I had never written a line but had stayed making pies in the kitchen. A lot of good savage work gets destroyed in these moods.'[32] The opposition in Harwood's mind between writing poetry and keeping house could not be clearer: the pie-making housewife is 'respectable', the poet 'savage'. This self-division causes an almost intolerable ambivalence which leads to the disastrous scenario in which she first destroys her own work and then regrets its destruction.

Again and again, Harwood's letters show that in her mind, meeting her own needs as a poet would mean neglecting the needs of others, and thus becoming 'monstrous' herself. She decided against republishing 'Burning Sappho' in her first book because, as she told Tanner, 'it might hurt [Bill's] feelings...Too nasty'.[33] It is to Tanner, too, that she confided her struggles to make room for her own work: 'I am fighting for time at present, never seem to have an hour or two to compose myself', she wrote in 1961. 'I need to have silence. But it's too unpleasant for the family if I take what I need.'[34] Ten years later, working full-time as a medical secretary as well as doing the bulk of the household labour, she would make very much the same complaint:

> I am defeated not by the grandeurs & miseries of time but simply by the necessary housework...I get tired, and as I have to go to work it is necessary to sleep...The only solution is a kind of selfishness I'm not capable of.[35]

The adjectives are telling: nasty, unpleasant, selfish. They are all highly pejorative, and all designate a potential failure on her part to put other people's needs before her own.

It is evident in letters across 30 years that Harwood experienced enormous inner conflict around this question of how to meet her own needs as a poet while not neglecting the needs of her family. '[Children] need a whole-hearted mother, not a half-hearted poet', she told Barbara Williams in a 1988 interview[36], though at the time she had raged in letters to Tanner at the loss of poems she did not have time to write, and insisted that her own 'talents' were just as valuable as those of her children. In the 1970s, she would adopt a feminist perspective – though only ever in private – to explain her own incapacity to turn her back on others: 'Women…(at least of my generation) have to escape their conditioning', she told Tanner in 1973, adding that 'it has taken me many years to accept my own gifts (some of them have been destroyed)'.[37] Even at this point, the 'acceptance' she speaks of is by no means as well established as her statement seems to imply. As late as the 1990s, she would bemoan the strength of her early conditioning: 'I wish I could / be mad and selfish', she says, in one of her occasional poems, but 'It's no good': her early training was such that even in her seventies, she still felt compelled to 'rise early and pay every bill'.[38]

Harwood's conviction that to do what she wanted – to follow her own desire to be an artist, and to carve out time for that – was 'selfish' and even 'mad' was deeply rooted. But at the same time, she believed that such selfishness was essential to the 'true' artist – that if she was to write the great work she believed herself capable of, she had to be ruthless. 'There's a sense in which an artist has to be *unmarried*, absolutely self-sufficient, alone with his impossible visions', she tells Tanner.[39] Despite her marital status, she identified with this solitary figure, wrestling with his demons. In her autobiographical essay 'Lamplit Presences', Harwood recasts the poet-versus-lovely-woman debate in these terms. 'I said once to Vincent Buckley, when we were discussing the tension in a poet between what he can do easily and what the demon urges him to attempt, "I would rather have been happy"', she writes. 'He replied, "But happiness can preclude the greatest joys."'[40] She adds that

If you are to be a poet you must immerse yourself in the shades, accept your own death, before you can praise the world and make some answer to the powers that will grind you small whether you challenge them or not.

In this formulation, it is 'the demon' who urges the poet to go beyond what is 'easy', and thus into the realms of true art, and it is this very urging that makes happiness impossible. If Harwood were content with what she could do easily – what she could dash off, perhaps, in the pre-dawn hours before a hectic day of child care and housework – she could settle comfortably into the identity of the 'lovely woman'. But she is goaded towards what is difficult by the demon, who insists not on mere proficiency but on greatness, and craves not mere tepid happiness but sublime emotion. This idea that the artist lives in a realm of extremes – of not only ecstatic joys but also desperate sorrows – is a settled part of the Romantic ideal, which Harwood invokes in full force when she depicts the poet as engaged in a heroic battle with 'powers' that will 'grind you small'. From this unspeakable combat, the poet will ideally emerge with a song of praise on her lips – but only if she is prepared first to face life's darkness.

Harwood was never able to resolve the tension between caring for her family and community and pursuing her own vocation: between the woman and the poet or, as she expresses it in another poem, between 'baby' and 'demon'.[41] She accepted the gender roles assigned by tradition and, as she was always quick to point out, found a lot to like in them. Nevertheless, they limited her, both materially and psychologically. Right through to her last illness, she seems to have found it difficult to carve out the time and solitude she craved for her work. When she was in her sixties, one of her sons bought a run-down shack at Marion Bay named Herongate. She became its caretaker, and it became for her what she called 'the only room of my own I've ever really had'.[42] In a letter to Philip Martin about buying a desk for herself, she explained that at home she worked in the parlour, 'on a corner of the common table', while her husband 'and his two computers and printer entirely occupy "the study"'.[43] But at Herongate, she had the whole place to herself. 'I feel delighted to have such a retreat,' she wrote.[44] She took 'favourite books and odds and ends that people gave me to furnish the place', and fantasised about living there.[45] In a poem, she describes it as 'A nest that I shaped to myself', where 'Alone, I invested in silence'.[46] Then one weekend when the place was empty, squatters set it on fire and it burned to the ground. On hearing the news, Harwood wrote, she was 'shaken to bits'.[47]

In a letter, she describes a recurring dream (also the subject of her poem 'Herongate') in which she returns to the shack:

I would be at the door putting the key in the padlock...
all is well, I'd think in the dream, the fire was a dream

and the house is as it was. As I opened the door I'd
see that my hand was a skeleton: I had died and was a
ghost returning.[48]

The obvious interpretation is that when the shack burned
down, she herself died – her true self, the artist self who,
at Herongate, had finally been able to discover the joys
and strength of solitude.

But this is too simple. Harwood may have struggled
to juggle her competing responsibilities to her family and
her art, but she did not want to be the grand, isolated,
masculine artist-figure of the Romantic tradition.
That she was able to name and own her vocation, to
insist on its seriousness and importance, and to forge a
unique identity as an artist all from within a seemingly
traditional marriage is her achievement. When she first
began writing poetry, there were no models of poet-
housewives. There was virtually nothing to indicate that
a woman could be a mother and also a serious poet. In
fact, conventional wisdom insisted that it was impossible.
Elaine Showalter demonstrates that in Victorian England
it was taken for granted that 'motherhood and writing
are incompatible'.[49] This was partly on purely practical
grounds: families were large in those days and child care
only available to the very wealthy (in the form of private
nannies, governesses and tutors), and a mother simply
did not have the time to write. As philosopher and critic
George Lewes explains, 'eminence' in any field requires
'steady and unbroken application', which is almost
impossible for a woman tending to the needs of young

children.[50] There were other grounds, too, however, such as those set out by one cultural commentator in 1862:

> It is very doubtful if the highest and richest nature of woman can ever be unfolded in its home life and wedded relationships, and yet at the same time blossom and bear fruit in art or literature with a similar fulness...The nature of woman demands *that* to perfect it in life which must half-lame it for art.[51]

What he is saying, of course, is that it is not possible to be fruitful both physically and intellectually. Bearing a child is the 'perfection' of a woman's nature, but it makes her incapable of art. Ideas about women's physical capacities were changing by the 1940s, when Harwood married, as science challenged such well-established furphies as the belief that if a woman studied at university her uterus would shrivel and dry up. But underlying prejudices about what Harwood called Holy Motherhood died hard. In her novel *The Man Who Loved Children*, Christina Stead has one of her characters, Sam Pollit – who is based on her own father – voice an opinion oddly similar to those of Victorian critics. Women, he says, in his bizarre baby-talk dialect, should not get the vote because they 'know nuffin! Becaze if they ain't got childer, they need childer to keep 'em from goin' crazy; en if they have childer the childer drive em crazy.'[52] In one sentence, he brilliantly captures the double bind facing women: those who did not have children were regarded as sad, incomplete and ultimately mad, while those who did were effectively nullified by them.

These ideas were part of the social world in which Harwood sought to make a life that could include both children and poems. Despite her regrets about the poems she could not write because of all the dishes she had to wash, she was very clear that she would not have changed the choices she made. With the benefit of hindsight, she came to see the time in which she was immured in child rearing – during which she suffered an almost intolerable loss of self – as bearable because it was temporary. In one late poem, she tells a harried father to hang in there: 'Look at me', she advises him, 'I've lived through it. You'll survive.'[53] Her poem 'Impromptu for Ann Jennings' suggests something similar: those intense years of child rearing can be hell, but they are passing. In other words, she came to terms with the threat to her own creativity posed by having children by recasting it as simply a stage in her life, from which she had emerged relatively unscathed. 'We have risen', she exclaims in 'Impromptu': 'Now we move where we will…We are our own.' What's more, the time she devoted to her children was not wasted, artistically speaking. From it she drew some of her most enduring poems – including, paradoxically, the poems she wrote about this very struggle. Nevertheless, she was not entirely indifferent to the inevitable squandering of creative moments. In a late poem, she speaks with obvious regret of 'how easily the muse can wilt'.[54] And in 'An All-Purpose Festival Poem', she writes with who knows what degree of sarcasm that 'it's no great shakes if Baby wakes / and the world has lost a sonnet'.

If she had had a less traditional marriage, perhaps fewer sonnets would have been lost. But this was all new territory for her – as for all women who aspired to be artists as well as wives and mothers in the twentieth century – and she had to blaze her own trail. I would argue that her biggest struggle was a psychological one: to see herself as an artist, to claim an artistic vocation in the face of enormous cultural disapproval. The Biblical story of the talents gave her a way to do this, a narrative she could pit against the dominant one in which a woman's only talent is 'to keep house'. Nevertheless, even this powerful story could not entirely vanquish her fear that by pursuing a career as a poet she was selfish, egotistical or in other ways monstrous. She could not exorcise this particular demon, but by acknowledging it, by accommodating the demon within herself, she was able to find a way to be both a 'woman' – in her own, traditional sense – and a poet.

The Dark Tower

Dorothy Hewett

In one of Dorothy Hewett's later poems, 'Lines to the Dark Tower', a girl moves into an empty wheat silo.[1] There she lives alone, entranced by the view of blowing grass and flowing river and spinning windmills, and weaving what she sees into a magical web, like a twentieth-century West Australian Lady of Shalott. But unlike Tennyson's Lady, she does not pretend to be indifferent to the passing parade. The moment a knight rides by – or, rather, 'some talker / …his helmet / hanging on the back of his head', or 'one of the silent watchers / ill met by moonlight / his eyes flaming underneath his visor' – she runs from her sanctuary, irresistibly drawn by the promise and the possibility, the drama and the pleasure, of love. 'I was always ready to be inveigled / out of the tower', she confesses. She is a figure for Hewett herself, who at 16 was as excited by the possibilities of her future as a lover as she was by those of her future as an artist. At that age, indeed, she saw no distinction between them.

Tennyson's poem had always been important to her. She says in an interview that when she was a child, Tennyson's *Collected Poems* had been a favourite book: 'it was one of those marvellous old books bound in embossed leather, with the illustrations, and I adored Tennyson'.[2] She learned 'big chunks' of this book by heart, including 'The Lady of Shalott', which would eventually come to permeate her own poetry. Each section of her 1975 poetry collection *Rapunzel in Suburbia* begins with an epigraph from Tennyson's poem, and the first of her own poems in the collection, 'Memoirs of a Protestant Girlhood', pays tribute to it:

On the yellow farm
floated like The Lady down a creek,
lying on my back the sun motes danced,
black cockatoos massed shrieking in the sky.

There is something satisfyingly anti-romantic about taking the Lady from her willow-lined, sweetly eddying river and dumping her in a creek beneath a flock of shrieking cockatoos. 'Lines to the Dark Tower' has a similarly deflating feel, replacing the 'four grey walls and four grey towers' of the Lady's castle with 'a wheat silo / stinking of mouldy straw / and blood and bone', and the beautiful Sir Lancelot with the dunny-man's son. Nevertheless, the romance of the Lady survives her transportation to Australia. We are left in no doubt that both the country girl who floats down the creek in imitation of her literary heroine and the teenager who creeps into the silo to dedicate herself to art are versions of the same tragic heroine: the Lady ensorcelled by her vocation, yet lured away by love.

For Hewett, Tennyson's Lady is unmistakably an artist-figure, sitting in her tower watching all that goes on outside in a mirror and weaving what she sees into a wondrous tapestry. She is also distinctively female. In Tennyson's poem, she is under a mysterious curse which decrees that she must never look at life directly but only observe its reflections in her mirror – a striking figure of the Western ideal of Woman as remote from and unsullied by the harsh realities of life. The Lady seems to love her work, but there are intimations that she is lonely. When 'bold Sir Lancelot' flashes into her mirror, no more than a 'bow-shot from her bower-eaves', she is dazzled by his beauty:

> His broad clear brow in sunlight glow'd;
> On burnish'd hooves his war-horse trode;
> From underneath his helmet flow'd
> His coal-black curls as on he rode.[3]

The Lady abandons her work to rush to the window and gaze upon Sir Lancelot in the flesh, and so unleashes her doom. She leaves the tower and goes to the river, where she lies down in a boat and lets the current carry her, singing, to Camelot. By the time she arrives, she is dead. Her beautiful knight, for whom she gave up all, sees her corpse and declares: 'She has a lovely face.'

As she makes clear in 'Lines to the Dark Tower', Hewett identifies with the Lady both as a woman who wants to leave the world for her tower, where she can focus on her art, and as a woman irresistibly drawn away from her artist's tower-sanctuary by the beauty and power of sex. She also identifies with the 'curse' that falls upon the Lady when she dares to experience life for herself, rather than simply to represent its reflection in her work. For Hewett, the curse is also death, but this is not the result of some mysterious magic. Rather, it is the result of the pain, destruction and despair that love unleashes. Death may be the result of the social ostracism the woman experiences when she transgresses social norms: she is attacked, humiliated and/or shunned until she no longer wants to live. Or it may be the result of the experience of love itself: the pain of losing love, of being rejected, betrayed or abandoned, may lead to death. Finally, there is the risk of violence: bold Sir Lancelot may turn out to be a basher, a rapist or even a murderer. In her creative work, Hewett explores all three of these ways in which sexual love can spell death for a woman. Safer by far, she suspects, to stay in the tower and devote herself to art. The problem with this conclusion, however, is that she cannot quite bring herself to believe that life without love is worth living.

The Arthurian myth encapsulates something profound about Hewett's sense of her vocation as an artist. Her fear was that the story was true, that life and art are incompatible for a woman and she would have to choose:

either a kind of living death inside the safety of the tower or the dangerous adventure of life outside the tower. Again and again in her plays, poems and novels, she returns to versions of these same questions: Can the woman leave the tower and live? Can she leave the tower and create? And if she chooses to stay, is the art she can create worth the sacrifice of the life she could have lived? These were not just abstractions for her. There is an overwhelming sense in Hewett's autobiographical writings that what is at stake is nothing less than her own life.

Among Hewett's papers in the National Library of Australia is a kind of diary she wrote in the back of a school exercise book in 1939, when she was 16. She starts in beautiful pen and ink, but soon switches to pencil. She begins:

Dec. 31st. Sunday (very hot)
I am pretty, but I am something more than that. All I want is to be a great actress and a famous writer. Sometimes I sing too, and I spend a lot of my time drawing women with slanted eyes and long tousled hair. People do not approve of me, but I fascinate them. I've been called disgusting with my hair flying all round my face. Red is my favourite colour, and I wear it often, and well…My teacher calls me a poseur and the girls think I am trying to be different. Some of them think I am a genius, and so do I.[4]

It is a statement of her vocation, one which makes it clear that being an actress and a writer is an expression of her identity, not just of her ambitions. She is an artist because she *looks* like an artist, dressed in red with her hair 'flying' around her face. She is an artist because she is reviled by those who do not understand her: an artist is by definition an outcast, though necessarily a fascinating one. Above all, she is an artist because she is 'a genius'. But even as she makes these avowals, she incorporates a touch of ironic self-awareness: perhaps she is after all not an artist but a poseur; perhaps she is indeed 'trying' to be different, rather than simply expressing her true nature. She acts, and she watches herself acting.

Some 30 years later, Hewett would give almost this entire passage to the character Sally Banner in her sensational play *The Chapel Perilous*, which depicts the fate of a girl with artistic aspirations in Western Australia in the 1940s. Hewett was quite happy to admit that the play was 'outrageously autobiographical'. In an interview she gave in 1973, she said that she wrote it because 'I'd come to the stage in my life where I wanted to come to terms with everything that had happened to me'. She was also insistent, however, that it had wider resonance. Sally was not only herself but a 'typical/non-typical character of the period', and through her, Hewett was able to explore 'what it was like to be a creative artist and a girl...in that particular period'.[5]

Theatre audiences found Sally shocking in 1972, just as Hewett's own 'audience' – friends, teachers, parents – found her performance of the girl–artist shocking in 1939.

From an early age, she seems to have been very attuned to the mythology of the artist, and quite enchanted by it. She wanted to inhabit the persona of the artist as much as to be the creator of artistic work. She wanted to be the mysterious woman in red whom people stared after, mused over, fantasised about. In her mind, this woman was never a wife, though she most certainly had lovers. Hewett had no desire to take the conventional path and become a married woman – though she couldn't wait to be a lover. As she says in her autobiography, *Wild Card*, she imagined her future self as a fantasy version of Greta Garbo, fabulously wealthy and madly extravagant in both love and life. 'When I grow up I will be a famous writer *and* a famous actress and live in a mansion called Fairhaven on the banks of Lake Stillfarden', she writes.

I will never marry but I will have many lovers and many children and many servants to do the hated housework. In the evenings I will lounge on a crimson velvet divan in the Red Resting Room receiving my lovers and the other celebrities in a cloud of incense under the wavering light of the candelabra.[6]

It is an impressively specific fantasy, and one that Harwood seems to have embraced at least partly because it was so entirely antithetical to the lives of the women around her. She knew what her fate was supposed to be: 'Girls got married and had babies and did the right thing and all the rest of it', as she put it in an interview.[7] But she also knew that exceptions were made for actors and other celebrities, and she was determined that she would be among them. In one of her school exercise books is an essay arguing that a woman of talent should not be expected to devote her life to raising children. 'Any woman who sacrifices her whole life for the well being of her children is doing something unforgivable, especially if she possesses any great gifts', she writes. 'Then it is almost a moral obligation that she should express them.'[8] It is her own version of the Parable of the Talents: a gifted woman has no choice but to foster her abilities, even at the expense of her traditional womanly role.

Her antipathy to marriage seems to have come, initially, at least, from her mother, who was unhappy in her own marriage and who told her daughters 'not to get married and have a family if you want to get on'.[9] Hewett did want to get on, and marriage held little appeal for her. She would live a bohemian life as an artist, complete with lovers and incense, in her own West Australian community, and she would win the admiration of all, even those who disapproved of her, by her boldness and beauty and brilliance. To her, the artist was an exceptional being, fabled in myth and romance, exempt by virtue of her giftedness from the dull obligations of lesser creatures, and endlessly fascinating. In particular, Hewett adored the trappings of the bohemian life – the indifference to convention, the decadence, the crimson divans. As she got older, her idea of the artist evolved beyond Greta Garbo to encompass legendary French stage actress Sarah Bernhardt, English poet Edith Sitwell, and floppy-haired scribe and pre-Raphaelite painter Dante Gabriel Rossetti. Indeed, she says in an interview that she saw herself at 18 as

> the reincarnation of the young Rossetti…because I saw this picture of Rossetti when he was young and…he looked quite dramatic and I decided I looked exactly like him. So I tore the picture out of the library book and put it up on the wall and decided I was him in female form.[10]

In *Wild Card*, she is more specific: it was Rossetti's 'long wavy hair and dreamy-lidded eyes' that reminded her of herself.[11] By this time she was at university, where she would change into her 'black slack suit and…black velvet beret', smuggled out of the house to avoid her parents' disapproval, and 'sally forth, playing my version of the emancipated woman artist'.[12]

But though, as she notes with self-deprecating candour, her teenaged self loved to play the artist, and to project herself as a dreamy-eyed genius, it wasn't all an act. She was also striving to become an artist for real, learning both to write and to perform. In an interview, she says that she had 'always written poetry, since before I could even write. I used to get my parents up in the middle of the night to write it down'.[13] She adds that her parents, who spent their days in hard labour on the family farm, were probably wondering as they rubbed the sleep from their eyes 'what on earth it was they'd spawned. But they used to do it'. They later introduced her to 'the rules of prosody' and tried 'to make me scan' – an experiment that outraged the young Dorothy.[14] But it spurred her to learn to read and write, so that she could transcribe her poems herself.

Because they lived on a remote property, Dorothy and her younger sister did not go to school until Dorothy was 12, doing their lessons instead by correspondence. Her correspondence teachers were supportive of her writing. 'The poems that I in particular used to write were always treated with great seriousness by the teachers', she says, and her poems and stories were exhibited at the Royal Show and published in a student collection.[15] 'This sort of thing I think sort of orientated me to the whole business that you could write, that it was important, that it had some sort of meaning.'

The family moved to Perth when she was 12, and by the time she was 15 it was generally accepted by her parents and teachers that she was going to have an artistic career. To help her along her way, her father introduced her to writers he knew of and took her to the meetings of a local writers group, where she met Katharine Susannah Prichard and Henrietta Drake-Brockman, among others. He also organised for her to audition at the ABC, in pursuit of an acting career, and she joined the Perth Repertory Club. At university, where she was enrolled in an arts degree, she spent most of her time reading, writing and performing. She writes in *Wild Card* that she read her way through the English literature section of the library, focusing on poetry and plays, and spent 'more and more time in my favourite place, the little sitting room off the Women's Common Room. Drowned in yellow light, with the Virginia creeper tapping against the diamond-paned windows, I sit there composing my endless poems.'[16]

Poems were not the only things she was writing. She also wrote 'an experimental melodrama', which won a university one-act play competition, 'a one-act murder mystery', 'a two-act lesbian love tragedy in blank verse' and 'a full-length melodrama'.[17] And then there was her 'experimental novel' in which 'all my contemporaries, thinly disguised, appear'. But her crowning achievement was winning the *Meanjin* poetry prize at 18. It was an extraordinary coup, and the revelation of the prize-winning poet's youth caused 'something of a stir'. But it also showed that, beyond the velvet beret and the theatrics and the 'Veronica Lake bob', Hewett really had a future as an artist. It confirmed for her, she writes in *Wild Card,* that 'I am a poet'.[18]

At the same time that she was cultivating her writing and acting skills, she was also cultivating her sexual life. Part of living the life of a bohemian was being sublimely indifferent to stuffy social convention, especially around love and sex, and Hewett was contemptuous of traditional standards of respectability. Her family was not religious and, without any Christian urgings to 'purity', she could not see why she should not have sex if she wanted to. In the words of D. H. Lawrence – words she would one day give to Sally Banner – she wanted to 'answer to [her] blood direct'.[19] Her sexuality was important to her, and she acknowledged its importance in a way that few women of her generation have done. In her autobiography, for instance, the development of her sexuality features as strongly as the development of her artistic vocation. The first chapter describes the plays she invented for the 'improvised theatre' she and her sister created and the poems she made up in bed. But it also refers to 'the first stir of my sexuality' when her sister, in the role of 'some male surrogate, bends me over backwards on the iron double bedstead to murmur extravagant compliments in my ear'. In this chapter, she comments that the fairytales she read 'are all sexual stories', giving the examples of Hans Christian Andersen's 'The Snow Queen' and 'The Little Mermaid'. And she touches on those two unmentionables, masturbation and menstruation. 'The woodheap will be the place where I masturbate and discover a clitoris', she explains. 'Menstruation will be God's punishment for these forbidden thrills'.[20]

Her body and its capacity for sexual pleasure are very much in the foreground, even though she is discussing the supposedly non-sexual zone of childhood. She is also clear about her interest in boys and men. That first chapter opens with a depiction of herself as a 'skinny ten-year-old' crossing the fields on her family's farm with a billy of tea, which she is taking out to a farm worker. 'I am very conscious of the eyes of the handsome Italian farm labourer watching my stump-jump progress', she writes.[21] In a poem in her last collection, *Halfway up the Mountain*, she gives another take on her childhood interest in this man, whom she calls the 'handsome Venetian', though the childhood alter ego she evokes here is presumably a little older than the girl in *Wild Card*.[22] 'In that sex-charged atmosphere / his eyes were always on me / wherever I went he was watching', she writes. She is magnetically drawn by the pulse of his attention:

> I wanted to go
> to be alone with him
> close in the cabin of the truck
> smelling his male sweat
> and the cigarette smoke drifting
> waiting for him to pull over
> into the scrub and take me.

This is typical of the way Hewett writes about herself and her avatars in her many autobiographical poems and plays. She wanted sex, loved the frisson of danger, longed to be ravished. She was not ashamed of desires that would normally – at least for much of the twentieth century – have been fiercely repressed, unable to be acknowledged, let alone shouted from the rooftops in a poem. Certainly, she knew, as a 16-year-old, that a woman's sexual desires could not be spoken, much less acted on. But she didn't really know why. She had often been told she could not be a writer, but had scorned all such advice – and triumphed. She could not see why she shouldn't treat with equal scorn the prohibitions on sex outside of marriage. Her first boyfriends introduced her to 'the joys and torments of foreplay without consummation' at around the age of 17.[23] And then she fell in love, and one night, 'lying out under the pines on the university oval, I [lost] my virginity at last'. She was enraptured. 'To be joined to another human being seems to me the ultimate mystery', she writes in *Wild Card*. The relationship was everything she had ever hoped for. 'We tell each other everything and he absorbs me so completely that I can't stay away from him.' He was her Heathcliff, she was his Cathy. But it didn't last, and she was left feeling bitter and betrayed. After that, she says, she decided 'to be a whore'.[24]

One of the reasons the relationship ended was that Hewett's parents found out she was having sex. Appalled, and determined to protect their daughter at all costs, they put her and her boyfriend under such relentless surveillance that they were never alone together. This was not the first intimation Hewett had had that her parents – and, indeed, society more broadly – were not prepared to accept her choices. While she was still at school, she had dated an older man and her parents, fearing things were going too far, reported her to the Children's Court. She was charged with being 'an uncontrollable child'.[25] At that time, minors accused of sexual activity could be taken from their families and put into institutions for 'wayward girls' – horrifying places, by all accounts, in which girls were treated like criminals. In Hewett's case, the charges did not progress; her parents were as eager as the young man in question to avoid any publicity. But for Hewett, to have been charged at all was an unpleasant shock. The intrusion of the law into her private life 'transformed our romantic idyll into a dirty little sexual crime'.[26] It was a warning, perhaps, about how far her parents were prepared to go to keep her virginal, how much her chastity meant to them. After they intervened to poison what she felt was her first true love affair, the dynamic in the family changed. Willingly or not, Hewett found herself pitted against her fiercely determined parents as she tried to hide her sexual activity and they tried to uncover it. Her mother, she says, monitored her activities obsessively—reading her diary, opening her letters, even checking her clothes for semen stains.

Up until this point, her parents had been her biggest supporters. Her father, who Hewett says was a shy man with no experience of writing or writers, had taken her to meet authors and editors, and done what he could to further her career. Her mother, though sometimes hostile to her eldest daughter, had always encouraged her to be bold in her aspirations and not let her gender hold her back. Now, Hewett's potential as a writer paled into insignificance. All that mattered to her parents was policing her sexual activity. During one confrontation with her 'demented' mother, she writes in *Wild Card,* her father 'rushes in, white faced, with blazing eyes, throws me down on the floor, kicks me, and calls me "a filthy slut"'.[27] The love, pride and support she had always counted on from him had been replaced with fury and revulsion.

The irony is that while her parents were doggedly focused on her sexual behaviour, they were oblivious to the existence of sexual advances – or, rather, attacks – that she very much did not want. In her last year at high school, she went on a 'camp concert tour' with the Perth Repertory Club. 'Driving back to Perth in the hired bus after midnight, I am sitting in the back seat next to a middle-aged actor I admire, a leading light on the theatre committee, when he starts to grope me', she writes. She was rescued when a 'motherly, middle-aged woman across the aisle' invited her to come and sit with her. Her decision to remove herself, she adds, had consequences. She was 'inexplicably dropped from the cast list' for the club's next play, and 'never offered a part in a Repertory Club production again'.[28] Three years later, while she was at university, she was invited by the ABC to rehearse 'for a leading role in a radio play'. After the first rehearsal, the Director of Drama, 'a gross sixty-year-old who looks like a bullfrog', called her back for '"coaching", [locked] the door of his office and [made] a grab at my breasts'. She threatened to scream if he didn't unlock the door, and made her escape, 'shaking'. Once again, this was the end of her hopes of acting work with the ABC: 'I am never cast for anything again.'[29]

These experiences are an uncanny echo of Gwen Harwood's of around the same time in faraway Brisbane: female performers, it seems, were considered fair game wherever they were.[30] They are also quite revealing of the social confusion and double standards around sexuality at the time. On the one hand, a 16-year-old girl was supposed to be entirely pure, without sexual desires or experience. On the other, she was supposed to be available for the pleasure of others – though always on the quiet. The assumption of these respected and authoritative men was that Hewett would engage in unwanted sexual activity in order to win their help and support in her goal of becoming an actress. As long as it remained covert, it was socially acceptable. But for her to express sexual desires of her own by having a sexual relationship with her boyfriend put her beyond the pale – and, indeed, made her subject to legal action by the state. No wonder she was contemptuous of her society's supposed moral standards.

After she broke up with her 'Heathcliff', things began to go wrong for Hewett. She discovered that she enjoyed having sex even when she was not in love, and slept with a number of friends and acquaintances. But she soon found herself getting an unpleasant reputation. When she did fall in love again, the relationship ended badly, and she felt helpless and abandoned. She also found that there was real, physical danger involved in her sexual adventuring. When she got involved with two soldiers on leave, to whom her parents had offered hospitality, one tried to strangle her and the other to rape her.[31] She was half-appalled, half-excited by the risks she took in going with such men to isolated places. A couple of years later, she would get into a car with a complete stranger who picked her up at a tram stop and drove her to a beach, where he tried 'to take me by force. I [got] out of it by talking like a blue streak'. Yet she arranged to meet him again and 'for reasons I can't explain, [kept] the appointment'. She was saved from herself, however, when the stranger didn't appear. 'I have a weakness for sexual adventures', she confesses.[32]

The physical attacks must have taken their toll. But she also found herself subjected to social and personal attacks that were profoundly shocking and painful. Not only her parents but also her social group and even her lovers seem to have turned on her. The effect of this is chillingly conveyed in *The Chapel Perilous*, which proceeds as a kind of trial, with various characters – including Sally's parents, the headmistress of her school, a clergyman, friends and several of her lovers – taking on the role of the judge. From the beginning, Sally is surrounded by accusing voices, and *Wild Card* shows that their accusations are drawn directly from those that were flung at Hewett herself. 'What an awful little whore you are, Sally', says a schoolfriend. 'She was a real trollop. She'd lie down anywhere and do it like a dog', says her mother. 'Whore, dirty whore', screams her father. 'She's the university bike', announces a fellow student. 'You're a randy little bourgeois bitch', says a disgruntled lover. 'The only thing that interests you is what you've got between your legs.' Most hurtful of all, perhaps, are the rejections by her lovers, the very men who had begged her to sleep with them. 'I can't love you after I've lain on you like a dog', says one. 'Why weren't you revolted, normal about it?' When Sally declares that she is naked once more – spiritually as much as physically – a lover tells her that nakedness is 'rather unattractive'.[33]

This was the way her society dealt with a 'bad girl', the punishment it meted out to those who flouted its conventions. In *The Chapel Perilous*, there is not only defiance but some bewilderment in Sally Banner. What had she done other than have sex? All she had wanted was to 'answer to my blood direct'. Now she found herself reviled by everyone. For Hewett herself at 21, things escalated when her new love left her for another woman. She felt utterly destroyed. 'I'm nothing', she writes in *Wild Card*. 'I'm unloved. I'm totally unloveable. I'm sick with pain. I can't stand it any more. All I want is to obliterate *me*'.[34] Deciding to put an end to it all, she swallowed some Lysol.

Shortly before her suicide attempt, Hewett found out she had won first prize in a national ABC poetry competition. 'I have arrived', she writes in *Wild Card*. 'I am interviewed on the ABC, my poems are broadcast on the Young Artists' programme, my photograph is in the ABC Programme Guide'.[35] It was her second major poetry award, and she was only 21. Yet the joy of this could not begin to cancel out the pain of her broken relationship and the loss of her childhood belief that the world – her parents, society at large – was on her side. She had tried the bohemian life, she had tried to be an artist and to live by what she saw as the artist's creed, and it had brought her to this. As she saw it, her sexual experiences were directly linked to her artistic aspirations: it was her artist's belief in freedom of body and mind that had led to her sexual adventuring. She had thought to live utterly free, to 'walk naked through the world', in Sally Banner's words, and discovered that it couldn't be done. 'The bohemian life is unliveable', she concluded.[36] Having survived her suicide attempt – her parents rushed her to hospital, where she had her stomach pumped – she decided that she was no longer capable of running her own life. 'I hadn't been able to handle my life', she would say in several interviews.[37] She suffered, in other words, a complete crisis of confidence. The bold girl who had believed herself a genius, capable of anything, was utterly cowed.

In the immediate aftermath of her hospitalisation, she made two radical decisions. The first was to get married. This alone shows how deeply frightened she was. She had always sworn she would never marry, but now she felt incapable of facing the world alone. The second was to devote herself to the communist cause. In the past, she had been devoted only to herself. Now, she would give her life over to something important, something with significance far beyond herself which would give her life meaning. These two things gradually drew her away from her bohemian past. They also drew her away from writing. Always, as a writer, her own self had been at the heart of her work. She used poetry as a way to reflect on, dramatise, recreate or move on from her own experiences. Now, she had lost faith in the self that had fuelled her writing, and inevitably her writing dried up.

In *The Chapel Perilous*, Thomas, the character based on Hewett's first husband, Lloyd Davies, presents communism to Sally as a way to escape from herself.

'The things that matter aren't our own little egos, our happiness, our satisfactions', he tells her:

> The things that matter are building a new shining life for everyone. In five years we'll have socialism. And you and I will have helped to build it. That's our immortality.[38]

It's easy to see why this vision was so appealing not only to Sally but to Hewett herself. She wanted to flee the confines of her own limited, miserable, impotent self, and how better to do this than by transcending that self? She was looking for a new way to live, since her faith in the bohemian life of the artist had been destroyed, and what could be more worthwhile than to devote herself to the betterment of humanity? Joining the Communist Party was akin, she would later say, to a religious conversion. She became 'a devotee of the death of the ego', which 'stood for all the negatives – selfishness, vanity, corruption, bourgeois individualism – therefore it must be rooted out and replaced by this selfless servant of the masses'.[39] Her own writing, the poetry and plays and novels she had produced with such facility in her teens, was just one more manifestation of the monstrous ego. 'I suppose that I'd almost accepted that it was more important to be a political activist than to be a writer', she would tell an interviewer many years later. 'There was always a terrible struggle to get time to write. It was considered self-indulgent and egotistical to want this time, to want to write.'[40]

Hewett was not the first woman to succumb to a sense that writing was an unwarrantable form of self-indulgence. Women were not supposed to seek work that would satisfy or extend themselves; they were supposed to serve others. As Showalter points out, while a man's work would ideally satisfy both 'self-interest and the public interest', work for women always meant 'labor for *others*'. If a woman could not fulfil her 'natural' vocation of being a wife, mother and domestic carer, she should find other service work to perform. Creative work was very far down the scale of acceptable occupations. 'The self-centredness implicit in the act of writing made this career an especially threatening one', Showalter writes. 'It required an engagement with feeling and a cultivation of the ego rather than its negation.'[41]

The attitude, so prevalent in the nineteenth century, that a woman who practised any kind of art form was selfish and egotistical was inevitably internalised by many women, and persisted well into the twentieth century. In 1941, for example, Australian artist Stella Bowen wrote of her sense of 'the effrontery of taking up painting as a profession'[42], while as late as the 1970s, US poet Elizabeth Bishop felt it necessary to apologise for the egotism inherent in being a poet. 'I think no matter how modest you think you feel or how minor you think you are, there must be an awful core of ego somewhere for you to set yourself up to write poetry', she told an interviewer.[43]

In Hewett's mind, it was this 'awful core of ego' that had led to her downfall, and she was determined to rise above it. The particular form of self-abnegation Hewett chose was not domestic servitude – not overtly, at least – but service to a high political ideal. She was happy to lay the whole disaster of her personal life on the altar of the communist cause, to rise above her personal pain in the fight for a better life for all. Nevertheless, she did not originally intend, when she joined the Party and began work as a journalist for the *Worker's Star*, to give up her own writing. She simply found that there was no place for it in her new life. The only type of writing that was acceptable to the Party was writing that pushed its ideological position, and much as she supported the Party, she found it almost impossible to write to order in this way. 'I have turned myself into a political creature and dried up', she writes in *Wild Card*. 'I can't write poems like "My Glorious Soviet Passport" or "The Railsplitters Awake", so I write nothing.'[44]

But despite her new faith, she did not entirely abandon her bohemian ways. She had clutched at marriage as a 'viable alternative to promiscuity', but with her new husband away at the war, she had a number of sexual encounters and 'adventures'.[45] When her husband returned, she told him of her affairs, and he responded with surprising liberalism. He believed in personal freedom, even within marriage, and Hewett writes that he never gave her 'ultimatums', and left her 'free to make up my own mind, to do what I have to do'.[46] In *Wild Card*, she recounts several occasions when they discussed her lovers and liaisons in an entirely unrancorous way.

Soon, they decided to have a baby. For Hewett, this was part of her drive to protect herself from the pain and despair that had prompted her to try to kill herself. Having a husband and child would, she hoped, provide 'a sort of bulwark against the world, if you like, that cruel world out there'.[47] But things were not so simple. Soon after her son was born, she fell in love with another communist, a boilermaker named Les Flood, and after much agonising decided to leave her husband and child and go to Sydney with him.

In Sydney, her life was still centred around the Communist Party. She was a tireless activist, starting a magazine for women, distributing communist literature, fighting legislation to criminalise the Australian Communist Party and campaigning against the atom bomb.[48] In other respects, her new life was very different from any she had known. Her family had been well-to-do, and had helped her financially during her first marriage, while her husband was getting himself established as a lawyer. Though she was not wealthy, she had never felt the need of money. Now, she and Les were living in Redfern, a notoriously rough area of Sydney, and she was doing tedious, poorly paid manual work in a textile mill to pay the bills. Many years later, she would say that the experience was good for her. Without it

I wouldn't have known what it was like to work in a factory. I wouldn't have known what it was like to go hungry. I wouldn't have known what it was like to have the electricity and the gas turned off. All those things.[49]

At the time, though, it was dreary, frightening and stressful — if also exhilarating and revelatory. She had three children with Les and, though they didn't marry, the life she lived with him was far closer to that of the traditional wife and mother than the one she had lived with Davies. She was no longer promiscuous, and she did all the domestic work.

Still, her real life was with the Communist Party and her work for social justice. Living in a Party house in Redfern, she opened up her home to 'the world'. 'The homeless, the runaways, the bludgers, the users and the dreamers all sleep on our floor and then move on', she writes in *Wild Card*.

> I cannot get enough of them. Typewriters clatter, voices murmur into the early hours over the spitting coal, the kettle boils itself dry and is filled again. I'm obsessed. I want the front door to be permanently open. I want to invite them in and fill the house with noise. I want the talk never to stop.[50]

But things were increasingly difficult in her relationship with Les, who was becoming violent, delusional and terrifyingly unpredictable, accusing her of trying to poison him and repeatedly threatening her life. He would later be diagnosed with paranoid schizophrenia, but to Hewett it simply seemed he was going mad. In the end, she fled to Perth, with her parents' help, taking their three boys with her. There, she began to write poetry again.

*

In an interview, Hewett would describe going back to Perth as 'somehow walking back on my own footsteps', recovering some aspects of her lost self.[51] She was 35, and her life to this point could not have been further removed from the one she had dreamed of as a starstruck teenager. Instead of a glamorous mansion, she had lived in a Sydney slum; instead of a life dedicated to art, she had slaved as a reporter, a factory worker and an advertising copywriter while working for the revolution. Towards the end of her time in Sydney, regaining confidence in herself, perhaps, she had begun to write again, though she stayed well within the Party's requirements for literature. In interviews, she would say that one of the reasons she had not returned to writing earlier was that she was simply too busy. She was working, she was organising, and she was caring for three young children and a de facto husband: 'I never had any time to breathe, let alone think!'[52] It was only when she started her job in advertising that she found herself with the opportunity to write. 'There was a typewriter in front of me again, I could snatch a few hours, you know, here and there', she explained. Her first foray into fiction was a short story based on her experiences as a factory worker. 'It was a fantastic liberation of the spirit', she would tell the same interviewer. 'I felt as if I'd stepped out of a prison into the wide world again!'[53]

It wasn't until she was back in Western Australia, however, living with her parents and returning to university to finish her degree, that she began to disinter the 'ego' from which her earlier creative work had sprung. It is possible to see a kind of symmetry in Hewett's life up until this point, an almost impossibly neat thesis–antithesis structure. She spent her teenage and early adult years living the life of the bohemian artist – the more radical, the better. But she spent the next 15 years or so in passionate conformity to a political philosophy, and to more or less conventional domesticity. The second 'phase' was a reaction to the first, extreme in just the same way.

Both phases nearly killed her. The first led to such personal pain she tried to take her own life, while the second ended with her crouching in terror in her bedroom while her de facto husband debated whether to kill her tonight or tomorrow. In the third phase of her life, she seems to have sought a kind of compromise – the synthesis – that would avoid the extremes of both paths. Somehow, she had to find a way to be an artist while holding on to her sexual and emotional freedom. At the same time, she had to be able to earn a living, be a wife and mother, and remain socially and politically engaged. It was a big ask. The issues she had confronted in the tempestuous years between 18 and 21 had not gone away. If anything, they had intensified.

Beyond the practicalities of supporting herself and finding time to write, she found herself facing the seemingly unresolvable problem of how to live the life of an adventurous woman while also being productive as an artist. In 'Lines to the Dark Tower', the girl who goes to live in the silo soon learns that if she goes with the whistling boys who were 'always hanging around / poking prying hoping to pick up / an easy fuck', she would find herself 'left crying / in the rushes with the boat / floating away down the dazzling river reaches'. She learns to retreat to her tower and submerge herself in her art, watching

> the light change
> the drip of rain down the glass
> the figures passing
> ghosts through the glaze
> weaving them all
> into the great web of being.

The idea is that she will be protected there, but when she finally closes her tower once and for all 'against a plethora of whistling boys', she finds herself wedded to death in any case. She yearns after her lost love – 'one kiss could bring my lips alive / one tear redeem my life' – and loses her sight in the absence of the 'luminous' light her lover had brought her. She finally dies alone in the tower, and her 'finger-bones rot / into the weave' of her great tapestry. It seems there is no possibility of a resolution in which the Lady can live: she can either leave her tower for love and die or stay for art and die.

It is a dilemma Hewett's poems rehearse again and again. The poem 'Lady's Choice', which follows 'Lines to the Dark Tower' in *Peninsula*, is spoken by the Lady herself. In this poem, she rebels against her fate:

So there he is in the mirror again
his armour glistening with tears or rain
and I am expected to leave the room
…
…but I'm not going.

She determines to turn her back on Lancelot and his 'pontificating' and give herself instead to her art: 'I'll get up early / work on my poems and thread my loom / won't speak to strangers'. But, alas, the only freedom this choice brings her is the freedom to

choose my end
not death in the town round the river's bend
but here cold-hearted alone in my room.

The poem shows the emptiness of the Lady's options: she can stay and be cold and lonely or she can go and be scorned and rejected.

Hewett discusses this dilemma directly in an interview with Jennifer Digby in relation to another of her poems, 'Grave Fairytale', which ends the *Rapunzel in Suburbia* collection. This poem draws not on the Lady of Shalott but on another mythical woman in a tower: Rapunzel of the Grimm's fairytale. Like the Lady, Rapunzel lives alone in her tower but, unlike the Lady, she has visitors. If she chooses, she can let down the long length of her hair as a ladder by which others may climb up to her. At first, her only visitor is the evil witch who placed her there but, in time, she lets up a handsome prince, too.

This is where Hewett intervenes in the traditional tale. In her poem, Rapunzel and the witch are two aspects of the same woman. Rapunzel lets the prince climb up to her, and once in her room he falls on her, his 'foraging hands' tearing her 'from neck to heels'. But the witch pulls Rapunzel away and leaps on the prince herself, giving herself over to him while Rapunzel watches:

> Crouched in a corner I perceived it all,
> the thighs jack-knifed apart, the dangling sword
>   thrust home,
> pinned like a specimen – to scream with joy.

It is a rape scene, and the prince is a 'bully boy / sick with his triumph'. Yet the witch cannot get enough of him, and she and the prince 'roll in their sweat' all night. Rapunzel lets her 'glowing prince' into her tower three times, though he makes her ache and bleed. The third time, when he is climbing down, she cuts her ladder of hair, sending him to his death 'at the tower's base' where 'A hawk plucked out his eyes, the ants busied his brain'. But now, without her ladder, she is cut off from the world. What's more, she has destroyed not only the prince but the witch, that side of herself that relished him. This powerful part of her identity is reduced to 'a little heap of rags' that Rapunzel kicks 'across the floor'.

In the interview, Hewett tells Digby that the poem is addressing the very old question of 'how the woman artist survives'.[54] It is based, she says, on a 'horrific dream', which was 'incredibly brutal and frightening'.

What made the dream so frightening, she explains, was not the violence but that, to escape from it, Rapunzel 'kills the sexual part of herself'. Rapunzel, she explains, is attracted to her 'bully-boy', but she is also terrified of that attraction: 'She enjoys it and wishes to be taken and is an active participant in the taking, then realises how dangerous this is'. She must protect herself, and yet the cost of doing so seems to be her own sexual pleasure. When Digby suggests that the poem would be frightening for men, Hewett agrees, but adds that 'it is frightening for a woman too: this persona is deliberately cutting off a whole area of her life for herself and she becomes the lonely figure in the tower'. On the one hand, she is a figure of appealing strength: 'she is now herself, full of power'. But on the other, she has lost something: 'she is de-sexed in a way'. There is no simple interpretation, Hewett goes on. 'You must make up your own mind yourself whether the gain is worth it. Or whether she really had any choice in the end.'

It was a question that was, for Hewett herself, undecidable. Were the peace and strength the woman artist would gain from shunning sexual love – abandoning her traditional place in the story – worth the loss of a whole domain of experience, encompassing both great pain and great joy? And if her life was at stake, did she have any choice? In the Digby interview, Hewett goes on to link this poem with another, 'Psyche's Husband', which explores 'the survival of the woman in the sexual world'. In this poem, Psyche knows only too well that sexuality, sexual relationships, can be damaging and dangerous, yet she cannot resist them. 'What do you do about [sex] if you want your own life?' Hewett ponders. 'Do you find the "peaceful kingdom" with the woodcutter who seems to be someone unthreatening, or do you opt for the full-on sexual being, the glamorous beast?' The peacefulness of the tame 'woodcutter' is conducive to art, while the 'glamorous beast' may tear you apart. But is life, is art, worth anything without the danger and the passion?

These were questions Hewett deeply pondered and, indeed, lived out for much of her life. Her early sexual experiences had led her to believe that answering to her blood direct could end only in disaster. Yet she could not believe that the part of her that longed for wild and dangerous passion was evil, like Rapunzel's witch, and deserved only to be excised. She could not accept a 'cold-hearted' life. If she needed peace to write, she also needed passion. By the time she came to write *The Chapel Perilous* in the early 1970s, she was ready to lay at least some of the blame for the terrible experiences of her late teens and early twenties on the society in which she lived. In the play, she says, she wanted to explore 'how difficult it was [to be a woman and a creative artist] in Australia, and the hang-ups and everything that happened, so that you became sort of comic, tragic, satirical all in the one breath almost'.[55] A woman who wanted to be an artist was 'laughable in an Australian context', she goes on. 'Australian boys couldn't be creative, let alone girls.' Her own experiences as a teenage girl – particularly, perhaps, the intense surveillance, scrutiny and judgement she was subjected to – were linked, in her mind, with her aspirations to be an artist. As a woman who wanted to be creative, she was breaching all kinds of taboos, and her society was not going to take that calmly. What she experienced was nothing less, she suggests, than an attempt to destroy her. 'I'm still very fascinated by what I would call the destruction – or what I see as the destruction of the artist in Australia', she says, 'or the attempted destruction because I don't really think artists can ever be destroyed. But the…artist sort of rises up, you know, like the phoenix from the flames and creates in spite of everything.'

This is how she saw herself in the period after she fled to Western Australia. She had survived, and she was finding a way to create, 'in spite of everything'. With her parents to help look after her children, she was able to enrol in a master's and began to write plays, giving herself a 'course in playwriting' by reading the works of modern German playwrights. She married again, and had two more children. She began to teach at the University of Western Australia. She was still involved with the Communist Party, but the incredible energy she had once put into her communist activities she now poured into her writing career. In 1973, she would tell an interviewer that she was not as productive as she would have liked, 'partly I think because I've got a very demanding job, I work full-time, there are still three children in our house and there were once five, I write plays at the same time, I write an occasional short story, I write quite a number of articles and critical stuff, [and] I used to run until fairly recently an ABC program on recent books in Perth'.[56] As well, she and her second husband, Merv Lilley, presided over a kind of literary 'salon', a focal point for local writers. And then there was her poetry, much of which seemed to explore the same ideas and experiences as her plays.

The second part of Hewett's life is less well documented, with the first (and only published) volume of her autobiography ending in 1958 with her return to Perth. If her poems and plays are anything to go by, however, it seems she continued to try to find ways to reconcile the voracious 'witch', and her longing for the dangerous ravishment of sexual love, with the 'Lady', and her artist's need for tranquillity and distance from the world of experience. She continued to find herself hauled to the brink of death by her sufferings in love — but she also began to insist, with increasing confidence, that she would survive. She would not choose between art and dangerous love, and neither would she accept the Lady's fate. This is dramatised in the series of poems in the 'Alice in Wormland' section of her collection of that name. In these poems, 'Alice' is powerfully battered by the end of an adulterous love affair and longs for death. Like Hans Christian Andersen's mermaid, she wants to 'dissolve like foam / on the shore'. Each time she survives, she knows she has found no permanent safety. In one poem, as she watches the Grim Reaper withdraw, she calls: *'Au revoir… / till next time.'*[57] Sure enough, a few poems later, another relationship in ruins, she is standing in the bathroom at midnight with a packet of pills in her hand wondering if there are enough to kill her.

> *O death*   said Alice
> *let me go fast & blithely*
> *& let him weep*[58]

As the days go by, suicide remains a constant temptation. 'I want to lie on the ground / dead as a doornail,' she declares.[59] In one poem, Alice identifies herself with a seeming tradition of extraordinary women writers who died before their time:

> would she
> walk across water meadows
> a stone in her pocket
> like Virginia…
> choke on a fountain of blood
> like Katherine
> swallow an overdose
> like Sylvia[60]

By killing herself, the implication is, she can join the illustrious company of Woolf, Mansfield and Plath. It would be, in a way, the ultimate proof of her credentials as an artist – better even than a black beret. For Hewett, 'madness' had seemed alluring back when she first went to university. Her psychology lecturer had asked to psychoanalyse her, and she was 'flattered': 'If I can't be intelligent, I can be mad and gifted. Everybody knows the gifted are crazy.'[61]

But much as these poems toy with death, there is also a countervailing rebellion. 'She will not   die for love', one declares, 'but live   bewitched by curious magic'.[62] Again and again, Hewett's characters consider but reject the Lady's fate. In her novel *The Toucher*, published when Hewett was 70, the central character, Esther Summerton, even enacts the Lady's final journey. In despair after being abandoned by her young lover, Billy, she goes down to the estuary, gets into a boat and lies down, like the Lady. Her intention is to 'run with the current out to the ocean' – not to kill herself, but to allow herself to die, if no lucky chance should intervene to save her.[63] As she lies 'in the cold bilge-water' looking up at the sky, she asks herself if she wants to die. 'I think so, but I don't want to make the decision', she concludes. As she floats, she thinks back over her life, trying to make sense of it:

> She had squandered her days on earth, dangerously depleting her reserves. Writers needed calm, order, protection, sameness, yet every time she had even approached this admirable state of stasis, she had deliberately shattered it. Why was she so perverse? What was it that sent her whoring helter-skelter like a being possessed?[64]

As fate and her author would have it, Esther doesn't die. Instead, she is 'grounded in the bloody reedbeds', where she is found by a neighbour, who tells her this was only to be expected 'with this pissweak tide'. Once again, Hewett has created a character who cannot resist her own wilder desires, and whose desires take her to the brink of death – but who nevertheless survives. It is a tenuous survival, certainly. Counterpointed with Esther's story in the novel is that of the much younger Iris, the lover and later wife of Billy. She is beaten and abused by Billy – even as he tenderly cares for the elderly, disabled Esther – and ultimately murdered by him. The very man who brings Esther to life with his sexual attentions puts another woman to death. And though Esther has survived her own half-hearted attempt at suicide, it seems pretty clear she would not have survived a longer relationship with Billy. It is evident that for Hewett herself, the danger of sexual relationships is still vividly present.

Hewett's last novel, *Neap Tide*, contains a similarly disturbing account of the murder of a sexually adventurous young woman, Lorelei, by a group of drunken men. Lorelei sees herself as strong and independent, able to take care of herself and her child, able to hold her own with men. But her confidence is misplaced. She joins a group of revellers on the beach at night and in a horrifying scene is gang-raped and left for dead. Like Iris in *The Toucher*, Lorelei is a counterpoint to the older heroine, in this case, 55-year-old Jessie, a writer and academic who is sexually drawn to man after man in the New South Wales coastal town she is visiting on a period of study leave. Towards the end of the novel, she meets a magnetically attractive man named Oliver, whom she knows by reputation to be destructive, dangerous, possibly murderous. Within a few moments of their meeting, he asks her to join him later so they can spend the night together, and she agrees. She goes to his cabin, but while she is waiting, she is accosted by another character, an old lover, and comes to her senses. She turns her back on this dark adventure and decides to follow her 'sensible' plan of going to Rome to try to reconnect with her daughter and grandchild. Meanwhile, the terrible fate of Lorelei resounds through the book as a kind of cautionary tale, a warning that the dangers of sexuality for women are utterly real, utterly serious.

Both novels suggest that the relationship between sex, love, art and death was preoccupying Hewett when she was in her late sixties and seventies. But though in these works two women are killed by men in acts of sexualised violence, no women choose to die. Hewett's central characters ultimately choose to live with their pain. Hewett herself apparently did not try to kill herself again after that one early attempt, though she was often in despair. It seems she was unable to resolve the dilemma she faced: the impossible choice, as she saw it, between art and sexual love. In a poem in *Alice in Wormland*, which was published in 1987, when Hewett was 64, a woman laments that her lover will not agree to live with her. 'Life will pay us out eventually / for not having the courage to love', she declares.[65] A poem in *Peninsula*, published seven years later, declares: '[Life] paid me out eventually / for having the courage to love.'[66] Taken together, these two lines seem to encapsulate Hewett's stance: you will be punished for not loving; you will be punished for loving. There is no neutral position, no preferred option. If you love or if you turn away from love, if you choose art or if you choose sexual passion, there will be consequences. There will be death.

The poems in Hewett's last two collections, *Peninsula* and *Halfway up the Mountain*, both published when she was in her seventies, bring a new perspective to her artist's dilemma. Hewett was quite open about her fear of death, and about how much she hated growing old. As she confessed to one interviewer, 'To grow old gracefully seems a very difficult problem'.[67] But there was more to her resentment and reluctance than a refusal to go gently into that good night. The woman in these poems is mourning not just the loss of her youth but also the loss of her sexuality. This is foreshadowed in a handful of poems in *Alice in Wormland*:

She hated the menapause [sic]
the end of that rhythm
left her askew forever
she wanted blood
a man's seed   swelling
her belly...[68]

Then in 'The Last Peninsula', in *Peninsula*, she writes about having a hysterectomy. It is, she says, 'the first brush / with death'. In a profound way, the loss of her uterus foreshadows the loss of her life:

I die and the lost womb
and the last light
and the dark mystery
between the thighs
goes with me

Given the importance of sexuality to Hewett's sense of herself, to her identity, it makes sense that the loss of first her fertility and then her uterus would have profound significance. All her life, it seems, she had been entranced and enslaved by sex – as the lightest, most momentary touch, or as the full-on clashing engagement of two bodies; as a mere glance of recognition or as a stormy, 12-year affair. Now it had left her and, whether she liked it or not, she was alone with her art. After so many years of being seduced from her tower by a whistling boy, she had been left in peace at last. 'I am an old woman now', she writes in 'Writing Poems in the Blue Mountains':

love and sex are impossible for me
nobody looks at me any more
nobody dreams lustful dreams about me.[69]

This was what she had always feared: dying in the tower alone, her fingers rotted into her web. Yet what she found was that neither love nor sex was gone. Though she was no longer actively sexual, she did not cease to

feel. 'If your arm accidentally brushes against mine //
my skin burns for hours', she writes.[70] In her mountain
home, she is still waiting, still hoping: 'Is it too much to
expect / that you will come again?' Though she insists
that she is beyond love and sex, many of the poems in
her final collection are poems of suffering love. The
difference now is that love is played out entirely in the
realm of poetry. For Hewett, love and art had always
been linked. Overwhelmingly, it was love she wrote
about. As she says in an earlier poem, 'Conversations':

> if I lose
> I write a poem about loss
> – & win. [71]

Poetry had always been the way she turned loss into
gain: suffering in love was transmuted into art. Now,
with sexual love behind her, poetry stepped into the
gap. It had become sufficient. 'With my books and my
writing to sustain me / I no longer wait for your step',
she writes in 'Writing Poems'. In her life, poetry took
on the role that had once belonged to the eager hope of
love: 'the poem is the reprieve / the chime the charm the
pardon'.[72] 'We [poets] are the ones who keep on going
/ through drunkenness death and disaster / writing it
down', she says in 'The Prawn Bird'. The sheer act of
writing, of going on, is 'something / preserved from
the ruin':

we are in for the long haul now
the unfathomable patience
the cunning pounce on the word
the phrase   the cry   in a circle of light
the unfinished manuscript waiting.[73]

In the end, poetry became what love was, what life was, encompassing all. While she could still write, nothing was lost. Everything she was, including a passionate lover, remained.

A Rebel and a Wanderer

Christina Stead

Christina Stead was always prickly about the idea of vocation. Indeed, she often insisted to interviewers that she had never had any such thing. Yet in her semi-autobiographical novel *The Man Who Loved Children*, she gave the character based on herself, 12-year-old Louisa, a potent sense of predestination. In one scene, Louie is cleaning her brothers' bedroom and dreaming of being an actress. Her father has just finished telling her that she looks like a gutter-rat, while downstairs her stepmother is grumbling about her 'dirt and laziness'. Her younger sister is about to ask her to carry down the slop bucket. But Louie is far away, 'declaiming…to a vast, shadowy audience stretching away into an opera house as large as the world'. Her conviction that she is extraordinary saves her from the catastrophe that is her home life. 'If I did not know I was a genius, I would die', she declares – but to herself alone. She is the ugly duckling, whose future as a glorious swan will, she knows, take her far away from the chaos and violence around her.[1]

Despite her denials, Stead herself seems to have had some such conviction as a child. When she was 35, she wrote to Nadine Mendelson, the young daughter of a friend, that writing was always going to be her work: 'I had decided when I was six or seven years old that I would be a writer and I never had any other ambition all my life.'[2] In letters and interviews, she describes herself as effortlessly literary, her abilities recognised by others before she herself had owned them. 'Everyone always said I was [a writer]', she told Robert Drewe. 'Teachers would tell me, "You're going to be a writer," and send me to the headmaster with my essays. Actually, I resented mightily being told what I would be.'[3] Yet, despite her resentment, she educated herself for her profession by rigorous reading, and as a teenager planned to follow in the footsteps of the great Goethe by studying at a German university. To this end, she began to learn German, but the intervention of World War I meant she had to switch to French, and so she decided to go to the Sorbonne instead.[4]

Such plans were highly ambitious for a girl from a working-class family with no money to spend on her education. Before she left school, Stead knew that she would have to work to earn the money to travel, and decided – or so she told Nadine – that she did not want to start her working life by becoming a professional writer: 'I wanted to have another way of earning my living so that I would be sure of my bread and could write freely in my own way until I felt mature enough to do good work.'⁵ As a result, she decided to accept a bonded scholarship to teacher's college – 'so as to have more leisure'.

This seems logical, but Stead's carefully hatched scheme did not work out as she had hoped. According to her biographer, Hazel Rowley, Stead enjoyed her years of studying to be a teacher, but her plans for a life of leisurely work and writing-on-the-side fell apart when she got into the classroom. She did not make it through her first week. Her voice failed, and she was temporarily transferred to a correspondence school on the grounds that the physical demands on her would be fewer. The problem cleared up, but as soon as she returned to an ordinary school, it recurred. The difficulty, it soon appeared, was not chiefly physical. Stead hated being in the classroom. Teaching was for her, as for her character Teresa in her autobiographical novel *For Love Alone*, a 'delirium of horror'.⁶

In later years, Stead would give several different accounts of what happened. In one version, the problem was not teaching in itself but being in an occupation that made high demands on her time and mental space. 'It wasn't the children', she told Joan Lidoff in an interview. 'I didn't mind that. But, your time is not your own.' In another version in the same interview, she related the problem more directly to her mental health. She didn't have 'the nervous strength' for the classroom, she explained. 'I have plenty of nervous strength for books. But all those little shrimps, no…I couldn't do it.'[7] It seems clear that, both physically and emotionally, teaching pushed Stead to her limits. The problem was compounded because she could not simply leave the profession and find other work. Under the terms of her scholarship, she had to work for the Education Department for five years, or else pay back all the money they had spent on her education. The second option was impossible – neither she nor her family could lay their hands on that kind of money – so she set herself to work out her period of indenture. She struggled on for a while, and then one Thursday morning, instead of going to work, she got on a train and left Sydney without a word to anyone.

Many years later, she would recreate this journey in *For Love Alone*. Sitting on the train, Teresa first thinks 'agonizedly' of the school she has left, of what the students and teachers would be doing at that very moment without her. But soon, her mood shifts and she begins to rejoice that she has found 'the way out, which alone does not lead to blindness, years of remorse and hungry obscurity'.[8] This was the future Stead herself feared if she stayed in her teaching career. She had imagined herself earning her salary conscientiously and using all her own time for writing, but she had found that her job was encroaching on her own time in an intolerable way. It was making demands on her she simply was not able to meet, and meanwhile her future as a writer seemed to be slipping away.

She seems to have made no plans for her flight. Like Teresa in *For Love Alone*, she took refuge with relatives in the country, but they contacted her father, who came to collect her. Though her escape attempt was so easily thwarted, it did at least make clear to everyone involved that the situation could not continue. Stead was taken to a doctor, who diagnosed her as suffering from a mental illness: neurasthenia, a condition associated with what used to be thought of as 'nerves'. As a result, she was declared to be 'permanently incapacitated' for teaching, and the Education Department waived her bond.[9] She was free to return to her original plan: find an undemanding day job to support herself and work on her writing at her leisure. She soon found a job as an office worker – she had been studying stenography at night, to equip herself for just such a change of career – and began to save to go to Europe.

This story suggests that Stead's sense of vocation was both powerful and inexorable. In her mind, it was central to who she was: she could not function if she could not see herself working towards a future as a writer. Having that possibility placed out of her reach made her literally ill. Something similar is suggested by a series of letters she wrote in 1942, when she was 39 and living alone in New York while her lover, Bill Blake, also a writer, was in California looking for supposedly lucrative work in Hollywood. Stead was working on the manuscript that would become *For Love Alone*, racing against an increasingly tight publication deadline, and her letters to Blake document her continuing obsession with her work. 'There is so much to write, that is the devil of it', she tells him. '[I]f the angel of death came to me right now, I would protest, "But, Angel, I haven't even written *one* book, my dear: and remember I was sent here to be a writer: you really have mistaken the date," and perhaps he/she/it would go away convinced'.[10]

In general, Stead was not one to speak of angels. She was relentlessly clear-sighted – or bitingly cynical, depending on your point of view. But the sense of destiny she articulates here is consistent with other private pronouncements she made about her vocation. Though she tells her imaginary angel that she hasn't written a single book, she had in fact published four at this point in her career, including her masterpiece, *The Man Who Loved Children*, which appeared in the US early in World War II to general indifference. All her works had been critically praised by a handful of discerning readers, but they had not sold well. Nevertheless, her ambition was great: as she once expressed it, her goal was to write something 'so good that there will be no denying it on anyone's part'.[11]

Late in life, however, having won precisely the kind of worldwide acclaim she had once dreamed of, she insisted on denying her vocation. When Lidoff, who was preparing what would be the first book-length study of Stead's novels, asked her at what point she had decided she was a writer, Stead pulled her up: 'I never decided I was a writer. I'm not a writer'. 'I never wanted to be a writer', she told a newspaper reporter when she was 80. 'I became one accidentally, because I could write.' To another interviewer, she went further, declaring that as a young woman, writing 'was nothing to [her]' and that she 'didn't give tuppence about writing'.[12]

Other such statements – so thoroughly contradicted by Stead's private letters – go further to offer an alternative narrative. Far from wanting to be a writer, she told Drewe, 'All I wanted was to find the right man and marry him'. 'I'm a believer in love. That's really my religion', she declared to the *Sydney Morning Herald*, which rewarded her piety by using 'Love is her religion' as their headline. 'I had no [writing] ambition', she insisted to another interviewer. 'My ambition was to love, meet and marry the right man.'[13] Clearly, in her mind, a life as a lover was far more socially acceptable for a woman than one as a writer and she was determined that everyone should know she had got her priorities right. The reality was very different, however. If she had really wanted only to marry, she could have done so before leaving Sydney – but only if she was prepared to give up her plans for the Sorbonne.[14] Similarly, if marriage had been her goal, she would probably not have lived with a married man – whose Catholic wife showed no signs of giving him a divorce – for so many years. Besides, for her, writing had the same force and power, the same instinctual energy, as love and sex: there was no question of living without either. Yet her fear of being judged unwomanly and humiliated on the public stage was profound.

According to Rowley, Stead's sense of being unloved and unlovable was seeded in her childhood. Her mother died when she was two and a half, and her father married again less than two years later. 'My stepmother did not like me', Stead wrote. 'Very natural, as I was the kind of child only a mother could love and then probably with doubts.'[15] She described Ada Stead's treatment of her as 'dubious' – to the point where visitors to the house sometimes thought her a foster child. But it was her father's treatment of her she most resented. He constantly belittled her, loudly bemoaning the fact that he, a handsome man, should have been saddled with a plain daughter, and making his adolescent sons – Stead's half-brothers – commiserate with him. 'Dad always said, "But she's so *ugly*"', one of her half-brothers told her late in life. 'Until one day I looked and saw you were not ugly at all.' 'For always I felt like a cripple', Stead reflected, 'because my father thought I was ugly.'[16]

Stead's childhood experience of her father, David Stead, is fictionalised in *The Man Who Loved Children*, which she often claimed was a 'word for word' account of her life in Watson's Bay with her family.[17] No novel, of course, is a direct transcription of reality. But there is little doubt this book reflects what Stead herself believed to be the truth of her childhood. The character based on her father, Sam Pollit, is a vain, manipulative bully, who spends his time 'poking and prying' into his children's lives, when he is not spouting his self-deluding, self-justifying rhetoric of freedom and brotherly love. He simply cannot hear what his adolescent daughter, Louie, is trying with clumsy tenacity to tell him. She is saying that he is strangling her, choking her, killing her with his obsessive surveillance, his appropriation of her every thought, his determination to make her serve him all his life. But such a view is entirely inconsistent with Sam's most cherished beliefs about himself: that he is a wonderful father, that his children are the luckiest children in the world, that anyone under his influence will become a shining example of virtue – unless, of course, there is some pre-existing evil in their soul, which is what he comes to suspect of Louie. Again and again, Louie begs him to let her leave, and again and again, he draws the net tighter around her.

It is an agonising experience for the reader, let alone for poor Louie. One American critic, Randall Jarrell, felt so shaken by Stead's portrayal of Sam that he found himself questioning masculinity itself: '[Sam] is so idealistically, hypocritically, transcendentally masculine that a male reader worries, "Ought I to be a man?"'[18] He was not alone. Stead said that men who had read the book would come up to her and say: 'It worries me so much. Am I like that?' Her response was reassuring. 'You can see they're not', she told Lidoff. 'The [ones who are like that] wouldn't worry of course.'[19] She was always adamant that she had drawn in Sam a true portrait of her father, and according to Rowley the correlation between Sam and David is precise. David's 'real-life character was sufficiently extravagant and infuriating to need no further embellishment', Rowley writes.[20]

Certainly, Sam taunts his adolescent daughter Louie in the same way that David taunted Christina, focusing particularly on her size. Stead was not fat, Rowley says.

Yet one of her brothers remembered that David used to call her 'a lazy fat lump'[21], while a friend recalled that even at 80, Stead could not disguise her hurt as she told of how her father and brothers had called her Piggy and Pig-face when she was a child.[22] In a letter from her late seventies, Stead says that she still got 'too angry with the old man (Papa) when I think of the dumb things he did'. One of these things was 'not understanding anything… about a young girl putting on flesh – you can't believe it, can you?'[23]

In *The Man Who Loved Children*, Sam doesn't like fleshy women, as his daughter observes. 'The swelling thighs and broad hips and stout breasts and fat cheeks of Louisa's [thirteen] years…were repugnant to Sam', the narrator tells us. 'He wanted a slim, recessive girl whose sex was ashamed.'[24] It is easy to see the real-life David behind the fictional Sam's distaste for – and unrelenting ridicule of – womanly bodies. One of the more obnoxious things Sam does is gather his prepubescent boys together to mock women walking down the street. 'As she walks she wobbles, boys!' he cries, drawing them all in to his conspiracy of contempt. The children take up the chant, with only Louie objecting.[25]

The message is quickly absorbed by Sam's daughters. Evie, not yet ten and her father's adoring 'Little Woman', feels embarrassed for her Aunt Jo, seeing her through her father's eyes:

She was very much ashamed of Auntie Jo's waggling; she feared that when her aunt went down the street, people would stop and begin to laugh, until the whole street would point at her aunt and shriek, 'As she walks she wobbles.'

Silently, she resolves that she herself will never be at risk of such a horrifying fate. 'When I am a lady with a baby, I won't have all those bumps', she tells herself. 'I won't be so big and fat, I won't croak and shout, I will be a little woman, thin like I am now and not fat in front or in the skirt.'[26]

Being 'fat in front' and 'in the skirt' is not, of course, the same as being fat. But such is Evie's horror at the possibility of ridicule that she determines to refuse her own womanhood. Louie similarly internalises her father's loathing and learns to despise herself. In one horrible scene, after a tempestuous run-in with her oblivious father, she starts 'bawling brokenly on the tablecloth':

'No wonder they all laugh at me,' she bellowed. 'When I walk along the street, everyone looks at me, and whispers about me, because I'm so messy. My elbows are out and I have no shoes and I'm so big and fat and it'll always be the same.'

Sam's response is to tell her to 'Go and put your fat head under the shower'.[27]

Louie's stepmother, Henny, makes everything worse, attacking the girl for entering puberty. She screams that Louie is a 'great stinking monster', a 'great big overgrown wretch' and an 'unnatural big beast'. More specifically, she decries the young girl's 'great lolloping breasts' and 'the streams of blood that poured from her fat belly'.[28] This last thrust is particularly vicious as Louie must have been entirely dependent on her stepmother for help in managing the practical aspects of her period. She is 'petrified with horror and pride', and her hurt is magnified when she realises her father will not intervene for her.

Sam's assaults are less hysterical than Henny's but just as deadly. 'What man will look at you with your piggish, sulky, thick face always gloomy?' he demands. 'Do you think any man is going after a face like that?'[29] When Louie displeases him, he does not trouble to hide his revulsion. Early in the book, for instance, he vents his disapproval when she does some ballet steps while her aunt plays the piano:

'Stop it, you fathead, you silly fathead,' cried Sam wrathfully, 'do you want to make an idiot of yourself? You don't know what you look like, you great fat lump. I don't want to see your legs: keep your dress down. And please tell Henny to lengthen it.' With a sort of sacred horror he looked aghast at her fat thighs half revealed.[30]

By the time the 14-year-old Louie has become the 18-year-old Teresa in *For Love Alone* – they are, Stead says, 'roughly the same person'[31] – she is skinny to the point of emaciation. 'Look at her!' exclaims Andrew, *For Love Alone*'s version of David Stead. 'Pale, haggard, a regular

witch. She looks like a beggar. Who would want her!'[32]
Fat or thin, she is unlovable. This, at least, is how Stead
seems to have felt. In interviews, she sometimes speaks
of both Louie and Teresa as though she is speaking of
herself, confusing the pronouns and referring to Louie in
the first person or herself, bizarrely, in the third person.[33]
She did not actually try to kill her stepmother, as Louie
does, she tells one interviewer – but she thought about
it. She did walk all over Sydney, as Teresa does, as part
of her efforts to save the money for her fare to England.
And, like Teresa, she did become dangerously thin. She
accounts for this with her 'privations', aimed at getting
her to London as soon as possible. To get to the fabled
English capital, she saved for five years, denying herself
adequate food and clothing and walking for miles every
day to avoid bus and train fares. Even after she arrived,
however, she found she could not bring herself to stop her
'privations' and as a result, she grew weaker and weaker.

Given her father's taunts, it seems possible she was
trying to eliminate the mature female form he found
so repulsive. Certainly, she seems to have believed that
the thinner she was, the more attractive she would be
to men. In midlife, she apparently told an interviewer
that Bill fell in love with her 'because he could count
my ribs'.[34] But there may have been still deeper motives
at play in Stead's self-deprivation. In her mind, self-
starvation was a form of rebellion and a sign of strength.
It was a visual signal that she had a different destiny, that
she was set apart. When she was in her late thirties, she
wrote a series of notes on the 'rebel', the woman who

will not conform to society's expectations – marriage, motherhood – but seeks a grander destiny. Such rebels have 'very little to eat', she writes; they 'don't even care so much for eating'. Indeed, their daring vision of a new world springs from 'the delirium of hunger'. The rebel's 'hollow eyes' and 'lean cheeks' set her apart from those who are willing to accept a good dinner as the price of their freedom: 'They believe that by their very perversity, weakness, nonconformity, they achieve more, go farther, are remembered longer than the good, faithful, patient.'[35] In this context, Stead's own emaciated frame becomes a badge of honour, the proof of her independence, the evidence of her difference.

Certainly her 'privations' were linked in her mind with her writing. In one interview, trying to explain how she came to write her first novel in London, she says that she was forced to it by the fear that she was so weak she might actually perish. 'I thought I was going to die, and I thought "well, I'll leave something behind me"', she tells one interviewer.[36] 'I was very ill, and when I came home from work…I started on this novel, you see', she tells another. 'It was just something I did almost without thinking, as it were. I'm not quite sure about those things.'[37] To Lidoff, she is even vaguer: 'I wrote it because – I really don't know why – an instinct.'[38] She seems genuinely unable to explain why, but it is clear that, in her mind, it was when she was in extremis that she began to write fiction.

*

Even after she had published several novels and made a name for herself, Stead's childhood experiences made her sensitive to the threat of ridicule, especially in her home country. In 1939, she wrote to the woman who would become her father's third wife, Thistle Harris, that she could not go home:

> home was so atrociously wretched and I was so ill at ease as a result that I do not want to see Australia, except on some gilded visit, if I ever get the gilding.[39]

She seems to be saying that she could bear to return to the village pond only if she could return in triumph, the beauteous swan dazzling all those who had so cruelly scorned the misfit duckling. Even under these conditions, though, she would want to be admired only from afar. She would not want 'to see Sydney, nor my family, nor anyone connected with the old days'. No amount of gilding, she fears, would enable her new identity to withstand exposure to her old environment. At any moment, it could slip away and she could find herself magically transformed back into the desperate Louie, 'a great vile blob of a fat girl covered with mud'.[40]

The mud she particularly feared was related to her marital status. She spells this out in a letter she wrote in 1942, when she was 40, to Bill, who had by that time been her lover for 12 years. His first wife was still refusing to give him a divorce, and he had been considering a move to New Mexico to try to expedite matters. In the letter, she explains that it is very important to her that they be legally married. It would make no difference to her commitment to him, or to the quality of their relationship, she avers, but it would make a huge difference to how she was regarded by others. If she never marries, she says, she will go down in history as '"Old-maid, Woigin". Ouch. This is terrible. No, Munx. I do not care to figure in history as a Woigin'.[41] Her fear is that if she and Bill are not married, there will be no public record of their relationship. She will be referred to in the history books as 'Miss Stead', and the assumption will be that she was unloved and undesired – worse, that she never had sex. This idea is too horrible to contemplate. 'If it was a choice between figuring in history as a Virgin and not figuring in history At all, I would at once choose, Not AT All', she goes on. 'Alas, such is my prejudice against purity. You are he who will save me in high school histories from appearing as a Battle-axe.'

Not even the glory of a brilliant writing career, in other words, could disguise the shame of being judged inadequate as a woman – plain, undesired, unwed. Rowley writes that for Stead, becoming an old maid was a fate worse than death: 'The unmarried woman stood to miss out on everything: sex, love, motherhood, and social respectability.'[42] Stead's notes on the 'rebel' – written in the same year that she told Bill exactly why she wanted to marry him – contain a detailed analysis of the place of women in her society. 'Little girls are promised a safe position in the conscript arm of marriage and child-getting', she writes. 'If they are submissive, good and neat, they will be admitted to society on the arm of a man. They will perform their greatest, their only social duty by producing children.' Their value will thus be assured, and they will receive the approval of all. 'There isn't a woman alive who doesn't understand all this in early childhood,' she continues, 'and is not perfectly aware of the ignominy, detestation, and social death that awaits her if she does not conform.'[43]

Nevertheless, she says, there are women who simply cannot conform. These are the women Stead calls the 'rebels' and the 'wanderers', those who set out to make a life for themselves outside of society's norms. They are objects of derision. 'Daughters who will not conform have no glamour, respect or love', Stead writes. 'They have no position in society – and what man will ever marry them?...and a girl not easily marriageable is just as ridiculous now as ever.' Much as she deplored this state of affairs, she could not pretend that it did not exist. As a woman who could never quite manage to be 'submissive, good and neat', who had no interest in 'a safe position' in the marriage 'army', and who was by nature a 'rebel' and a 'wanderer', she knew perfectly well that she was risking punitive action. In this context, it's easy to see her lifelong concern with her reputation as an attempt to counter the attack she knew must have been coming. In those interviews in which she gives pious accounts of her dedication to love and her indifference to any kind of writing career, she is trying to pre-empt any characterisation of her as a dried-up old maid. In her mind, she is writing the script for the high-school history books, and there is no way she is going to appear as that figure of fun, the old battleaxe of a spinster.

As an alternative, she offers the image of the happily married, sweetly domestic woman. In her entry in a 1942 publication, *Twentieth Century Authors*, she lists her 'hobbies' as 'fine embroidery, housework and natural history'.[44] Though she did have an interest (hardly at the level of a hobby) in natural history, 'fine embroidery' appears to be a complete fabrication – certainly she never mentions it in any of her letters. As for housework, she considered it to be the natural enemy of the writer. Her dislike of wasting her time on housework was one of the reasons she and Bill spent so much of their life together in hotels and bedsits. 'We always talk about having a home, when we get to the hotel stage', she wrote to a friend in 1950. 'But the fact is, the minute I'm surrounded by "the home"...I get practically nothing done. While here, friend of the threadbare carpet, I work and work every day, regular hours.'[45] When they did live briefly in a house (or, rather, a cottage), she complained bitterly about the demands on her time. 'I have been held up myself – various ridiculously small, petty things – well, housework is one of them', she wrote to a friend in 1967. 'It falls to me – rather a big place in my life.' The problem of the daily work required to maintain a household was 'insoluble', she went on, 'at least for a woman'.[46] To another friend she declared that 'Every person, every visitor, every house [is] a folly when they take your time'.[47] The truth was, Stead felt sorry for women who devoted themselves to domestic life. To her, the 'well-fed, jolly' conscripts in the marriage army were 'like animals in their cages'.[48] As a 'rebel', she was never going to accept that fate.

Nevertheless, her rebellious life was to be her secret. In public, she was determined to be as 'good and neat' as she could manage, and this meant insisting on her amateur status. 'I was never a professional writer', she says in a video interview. 'I never, never depended on literature to make a living. That seems even to me a shocking idea in a way'.[49] 'This thing, professionalism, I don't like that', she scolds Lidoff.[50] This was completely untrue. In her letters, she speaks of herself as a professional from the beginning – in fact, she prides herself on her professionalism. Far from being shocked by the very idea of making money from writing, she had always hoped to be able to support herself through her fiction. Even before her first book was published, she was hoping to make 'a little money' from it.[51] And once her books started to appear, she had every intention of becoming a professional writer. 'We must work at writing as a profession[,] a trade, seriously, taking risks and living quite cheaply until we begin to make a small yearly income', she wrote to Bill in 1942. In the same year, she noted, 'I am not a bit satisfied with the bit of work I have done so far – so few books. I have got to make a good living and not by obeisance, simply by production; it can be done'.[52] At 78, she was happy to admit the subterfuge to an old friend, explaining that though her time was taken up with 'all sorts of stuff connected with my "profession,"' she refused to acknowledge her professional status: 'I'm an amateur, I insist'.[53]

In the same way, she denied that she had any kind of work ethic, declaring with insouciance that she had 'no special feelings about writing, about having to write'.[54] In fact, her working life was gruelling, as she points out in a 1958 letter. 'I sweat blood over [my novels] and write and rewrite and rewrite...I make for each one a thousand plans — plans of motive, action, intention and what not.' In another letter she notes that she 'can rewrite a short thing 20 times; cunningly I hope — so that it does not appear'.[55] But in interviews, she was adamant that she never planned her books and neither rewrote nor revised. 'Never ever?' an intrepid reporter persists. 'Never', Stead avers. 'Bores me stiff.'[56] Even the role Bill played in her writing was dismissed. In her letters, she refers often to Bill's comments on her drafts, and his views of her plots and characters. In one letter, for instance, she mentions that he is 'going through' her latest manuscript, 'saying "You said that fourteen times before" etc. He is really a wonderful help and an angel. All this takes place without my tearing out his hair or mine. Miraculous, but true'.[57] Yet she tells one interviewer that she and Bill 'never mentioned our books to each other' and another that 'We never, never discussed that stuff with each other'.[58]

One baffled interlocutor suggests, after fruitless questioning about her process and techniques, that Stead's writing was 'almost like automatic writing'. Stead gives this gambit her qualified approval: 'It's not automatic, but it's a thing that comes out by itself.'[59] If she could create the impression that she was a natural artist whose great works simply flowed forth, independent of any will of hers, she could account for the anomaly of being a seemingly happy woman who wrote books. For it was an anomaly. Elaine Showalter easily demonstrates that in the nineteenth century 'one of the most persistent denigrations of women novelists was the theory that only unhappy and frustrated women wrote books'.[60] The idea was that a 'normal' woman would find happiness in 'that sweet domestic and maternal sphere to which her whole being spontaneously moves', as George Lewes put it in 1852. Only if she was shut out from that sphere by 'thwarted affections' – in other words, if she could not find a husband and/or have children – would she turn 'to literature as to another sphere'. Showalter gives numerous instances of this view, which was the dominant one in the second half of the nineteenth century. 'Women who are happy in all home-ties and who amply fill the sphere of their love and life, must, in the nature of things, very seldom become writers', pronounced Gerald Massey in 1862, while Catherine J. Hamilton wrote in 1892 that 'Happy women, whose hearts are satisfied and full, have little need of utterance'.[61]

The assumption was that a successful writer was by definition an unsuccessful woman. This view went virtually unchallenged, in public, at least, for much of the twentieth century (Virginia Woolf's *A Room of One's Own* is a notable exception). In the 1960s, for instance,

Anthony Burgess began an essay on Brigid Brophy with the following story:

> An American professor of mine, formerly an admirer of Miss Brophy's work, could no longer think of her as an author once he'd seen her in the flesh. 'That girl was made for love,' he would growl.[62]

A beautiful woman could not be an author, it seemed. The argument also went the other way. In the 1950s, Elizabeth Hardwick commented, in relation to Mary McCarthy, that for a woman to be successful as a critic she had to have not only 'confidence and indignation' but also 'A great measure of personal attractiveness and a high degree of romantic singularity'. Without these, she was unable to 'step free of the mundane, the governessy, the threat of earnestness and dryness'.[63] A plain woman could not be an author, it seemed.

Comments like these, which appeared in the serious literary newspapers as well as in anthologies of criticism, were part of the air Stead breathed. She was very aware that as a woman writer, she would be judged on her looks. In 1944, when she was 42, she complained to Bill about the publisher's choice of author photographs for the cover of *For Love Alone*, admitting that she had thrown 'a three-ring circus' over them. The photos were, she says, 'grotesques', and 'frankly I would rather the book did not come out than that they should use those revolting pictures'. Her objection is not pure vanity. 'A book about love-affairs of a young girl and unfortunate love-affairs at that and you give a picture of the female author looking like a peculiarly untalented Notre Dame gargoyle', she goes on. 'This is not a joke.'[64]

Her concern is that her looks will undermine the credibility of her work. Without what Hardwick calls a 'great measure of personal attractiveness' on display in her jacket photograph, Stead will be written off as 'governessy', 'earnest' and 'dry' – and her book will be dismissed as the work of a desiccated old maid. Only an attractive woman could have something to say about love worth listening to. Even worse, perhaps, for Stead would be the assumption that as a 'gargoyle', she had turned to writing only because nobody wanted to marry her, and thus she had been unable to fulfil her 'natural' calling to wife- and motherhood.

This view of women writers has been surprisingly persistent. Paul Johnson's 2006 book *Creators,* which discusses nineteenth-century women writers exclusively in terms of their looks and marital status, rehearses the very same arguments Showalter identifies. Johnson speculates on mysteries such as how a woman as physically repulsive as George Sand could have scored such a good-looking celebrity lover as Chopin, and assures the reader that George Eliot's 'equine' countenance and freakishly small head prevented her from making a marriage in which 'she might have been perfectly happy, given birth to many children, and never written a novel'.[65]

For Stead, the prospect of being discussed in such terms must have been horrifying. It would have seemed an agonising echo of her father's long-ago taunts that no man would ever want her. 'We were brought up to be pretty and catch men', she tells an interviewer. 'I wasn't pretty and they didn't think I'd catch one'.[66] Her life had proved 'them' wrong: plenty of men had found her attractive, and she had 'caught' more than one. Little wonder that she wanted to crow about this, particularly when such crowing would help to counterbalance any portrayal of her as 'Old-maid, Woigin'. (She and Bill finally married in 1952.) In her seventies, she spoke proudly in her correspondence of her trunkful of love letters, and dropped hints about men who were interested in her. 'You wouldn't believe it of an old chick like me', she writes to Nadine, 'but life continues to surprise little girls, *especially* the plain ones, who are taught they must expect nothing of LIFFEY (as Bill called life, for a joke).'[67] It was an ongoing satisfaction to her that men had loved her, and still loved her. In one letter, she apologises to a friend for talking 'too much about my men friends', explaining that it is not 'bragging' but wonderment: 'I am so staggered and delighted that they even look at me!'[68] To Stead, her love affairs were worth singing about. Her writing, on the other hand, would not win her any admiration as a woman, and might even raise doubts about just how womanly she was.

In her own mind, however, love and writing were intimately interrelated, part of the same survival instinct, and originating in the very roots of the self. 'Writing is creative, love is creative. It's exactly the same', she once told an interviewer. To another, she drew an analogy between writing a story and falling in love. 'The start of a story is like a love affair, exactly', she told Jonah Raskin. 'It's like a stone hitting you. You can't argue with it.' Similarly, she told Graeme Kinross-Smith that her novels 'usually begin with a person...I think, ah, he'll develop, he's the one, just as in a love affair'.[69] For her, vocation was a force akin to sex in its primal power – and as impossible to discipline. Indeed, in one early letter, she explicitly makes this connection, saying that writing is 'a need, a frightful desire, stronger than any other physical desire' and comparing it to 'the passion, energy and struggle, the night of which no one speaks, the creative act'.[70] As a writer, she was also very much a lover.

Yet she did not expect the non-artists of the world to understand this. As late as the early 1980s, she felt that, like all women, she would be judged primarily on her looks and her love-life – and in this she was not entirely wrong. In 1983, the writer of her obituary in *The Times* felt it necessary to include a description of her, purportedly from the 1940s, as 'tall, plain, quiet, intense, brown-haired'.[71] How Stead would have hated that slipped-in slight, though it may have been mitigated for her by the inclusion of her incomparably ladylike hobbies: 'She enjoyed fine embroidery and natural history when she was not writing', *The Times* assures us.

Ten years later Rowley, in her acclaimed biography of Stead, would give a peculiar emphasis to the question of Stead's looks in the prominence she accords to the views of critic Clifton Fadiman, a champion of Stead's writing who met her briefly in New York in 1936. Fadiman told Rowley that Stead 'was simply *not* a handsome or pretty woman', and went further to deduce that her lack of physical attractiveness was 'at war with what I really believe was her deepest wish – to be loved romantically, almost in the nineteenth century tradition'.[72] Fadiman's view – based on this one meeting – seems to have made an impression on Rowley, who, later in the biography, states as her own opinion the conviction that 'Stead's deepest longing was to be romantically courted by men'.[73] She does not perpetuate Fadiman's oddly naïve assumption that only beautiful women are lovable. But by insisting that what Stead most wanted was romantic love, she buys into Stead's own mythology of herself quite as much as *The Times* with its allusion to her imaginary passion for needlework. The title of Stead's fifth published work, *For Love Alone*, may have been a factor in this. But this title – which Stead did not choose and always distanced herself from – is misleading: Stead's autobiographical heroine Teresa is clearly driven by something other than her search for love. In her notes for the book, Stead ruminates on Teresa's motivation: 'It was not home, food, clothes and love, she wanted – som[e]thing else – learning, passion, to succeed in her desire (whatever it happened to be).'[74]

Stead was the same. She loved being in love, there is no doubt. But it was not her 'deepest longing'. Her sense of herself as a writer was at least as strong – or, rather, was in some way a part of her sense of herself as a lover.

When she was in her sixties, she told an interviewer that writing was her morality: 'When I'm writing – it doesn't matter what I'm writing...I'm in tune with everything. Everything's going properly. That's moral, to me'.[75] When she could not write, she was miserable. 'If only I could get to some writing', she told a friend in 1975, when she was 73, 'all troubles would fly away like the sea-clouds which are always floating fast over this area'.[76] For her, her writer's vocation was at the heart of her identity, her mental health, her happiness and her loves – but this was a private truth, not for those who could not be expected to understand. In public, she insisted on being first and foremost a lover, and only secondarily, accidentally, incidentally, a writer.

A Working Writer

Ruth Park

The question of vocation takes centre stage in the two volumes of Ruth Park's autobiography, *A Fence Around the Cuckoo* and *Fishing in the Styx*. From earliest childhood, Park writes, she knew she would be a writer: 'It had been as if a voice spoke from a burning bush.'[1] Her depiction of her vocation to the literary life contains all the classic elements of the artist's call: it came out of nowhere, it was a summons that could not be set aside or ignored, and it shaped her destiny. Normally, however, this call takes shape in a specific cultural context: the little girl who longs to be a writer begins her life as a passionate reader surrounded by books, and as part of a family or society that holds writers (in the abstract, at least) in high esteem. Park's context was very different. According to *A Fence Around the Cuckoo*, for the first ten or so years of her life, she had no books, and no access to books. In the early 1920s, her father was part of a work gang that travelled around remote parts of the North Island of New Zealand building roads and bridges, and until she was six years old her home was a tent. Neither her father nor her seamstress mother owned any books. Even when the family settled in the tiny town of Te Kuiti, where Ruth would go to school, books were in short supply. As Park writes in *Fence*, 'No one I knew had any books.' The irresolvable problem of poverty was compounded in the wider community by a moral distrust of all that books stood for. As Park explains, 'It was thought that reading poked your eyes out and kept you from doing wholesome things.'[2]

Nevertheless, Park insists that from her earliest years – before she had ever so much as set eyes on a book – she wanted to be a writer. She is a little vague on exactly what she understood by this term as a child, but it was clearly connected with storytelling. Her father, she says, was an 'entrancing storyteller', and told her 'the savage hero tales of his ancestral land', Scotland, which she would act out on her own in the New Zealand bush:

> I had to be every character: William Wallace, executed on Tower Hill; the black-hooded executioner with his fan-shaped axe, wicked King Edward strutting triumphantly; Wallace's brave daughter climbing up Traitor's Gate to take away her father's head. My mother said my dialogue could be heard for half a mile.[3]

She had other sources of stories, too. By the time she started school – having already, precociously, learned to read and write – she was familiar with 'newspapers, public signs and the interesting information on golden syrup tins and packets of Amber Tips tea'.[4] It was the children's pages of the *New Zealand Herald* that most entranced her. Her first literary role model, she writes, was Elsie Morton, editor of those much-prized pages. 'I revered her as if she were George Eliot', Park explains. 'She also wrote a column for the Saturday supplement, my major reading material, and I admired it so much I learned some of her text by heart.'[5]

The reference to George Eliot is revealing. In wealthier homes in New Zealand and England and the US, little girls were devouring *The Mill on the Floss* and *Middlemarch* and dreaming of becoming novelists when they grew up. Harwood read Homer and Milton as a child, Hewett immersed herself in Tennyson and Rossetti, Stead read her father's works of natural science and his collections of the novels of H. G. Wells, Aldous Huxley and Herman Melville. All were reading works firmly entrenched as high culture – works of Literature – and taking as their role models men who were highly revered as Artists. Park's key childhood texts, by contrast, were newspaper stories, and her role model a local editor and columnist. Her vocation was formed in the context of a very different set of personal and cultural imperatives, and as a result her sense of herself as a writer was an unlikely mix of the lofty ideals of the artist so familiar from Romanticism and the pragmatic incarnation of those ideals in popular writing for commercial purposes. Park seems always to have seen herself as a professional writer: she had no choice but to earn her own living, and since she had very few careers open to her, she determined to make writing her job. At the same time, she had the highest possible conception of her work as a vocation. As she told D'Arcy Niland on the eve of their marriage, 'I need to be a writer, that's what I need from life'.[6]

She wanted to write, she makes clear, because she loved stories and storytelling, because there was something inside her that needed to find expression in words on a page, and because it was her destiny. As she once told an interviewer, 'You have to serve the god. Even if you have only a tiny bit of talent, you have to do that.'[7] She understood her vocation in terms of the ideal of the artist, in other words, but she lived it out in the very different conditions of the professional writer. In her autobiography, writing of her sense of herself as a writer, she weaves these two strands together with great ingenuity – but at times the resulting thread begins to fray. On the one hand, she insists that she has had the incredible good fortune of being able to turn her great passion into a successful career; on the other, she records a lack of fulfilment in her writing life that she cannot account for. The unspoken and perhaps inadmissible sub-text to her autobiography is that despite having devoted herself to writing, she has not been able to live out her vocation.

★

Park's earliest career aspiration was to appear in the children's pages of the *Herald*. By the age of eight, she was sending off stories and poems, and achieved her first publication at 11. 'It went straight to my head', she would say in an essay. 'I saw my life's work laid out before me, and have never stopped writing since.'[8] But to become a writer, she needed an education, and that was no easy matter for a girl of her class. The nuns at her primary school coached her for the scholarship exam that would enable her to go to high school, and she passed easily. But before she could take up her place, her father fell ill and the family found themselves without an income. With the Great Depression beginning to bite, life was becoming perilous even for those with a job. The Parks lost everything, and were forced to move in with relatives in Auckland just to have a roof over their heads. In such circumstances – there was no money for food, let alone for school uniforms and pencils and textbooks – Ruth's mother would not hear of her taking up her scholarship. When her mother told her she would not be going to high school, Park says she almost fainted: 'I thought I was going to drop dead. The air filled with black gauze.'[9] For her, it was a catastrophe. She had lost her home when they left the King Country, and on top of that her father was seriously ill, and food and clothing were in short supply. Now she was losing her chance to be a writer – for she could not see how she could be a writer without an education. Always cold and hungry, she began to get sick. 'Though I had always been so healthy as a trout, now I caught every infection that ravaged the half-starved town', she writes. 'Boils, abscesses, styes, earache, and a painful cough.'[10]

She began to recover from her misery when she discovered the Auckland public library. Though she could not borrow books – borrowing privileges were extended only to rate payers – she could spend whole afternoons burrowing into the reference section. 'For the first time in my life I had access to real books, classics, poetry, non-fiction', she writes. 'I got drunk on those books, staggering home in the freezing spring afternoons scarcely knowing where I was.'[11] It was her first contact with capital-L literature: 'Now I could read Homer, Emerson, Browning, Francis Bacon, John Clare and Gerard Manley Hopkins, who surely must have crept into that dusty impoverished library by mistake.' Her response was 'a certain madness...all of a sudden bemused by literary genius, dazzled and blinded. I copied long extracts of prose, learned poems by heart, reciting them as I walked home in a trance of bliss and excitement'.[12] She was for the first time entering seriously into her literary apprenticeship.

At the same time, her optimism began to reassert itself. Her parents had managed to get her 'a big six-penny writing pad' for her birthday – her heart's desire – and she 'developed a new style of writing; very tall, skinny letters, so I could get more words to the line'.[13] She continued to send stories and poems to the *Herald*, and to be published there. Her dismay when she learned she was to be sent to live with a distant aunt at Glen Afra faded when an uncle gave her a big sheaf of government forms whose blank backs were invitations to compose new stories. 'The excitement! Life changed immediately', she writes. 'My heart filled with hope and my head, instantly reacting, with ideas.'[14] At Glen Afra, nothing mattered except what she called her 'Work': 'I wrote every spare minute, continuing at night by candlelight.'[15] What she was writing was 'fiction, as imaginative as possible'.[16] It was an escape for her in two ways: it took her out of herself and into the fictional worlds she was creating, and it helped her to believe once more in her own future as a writer.

She was not in exile for long, and when she returned to her family in Auckland things had improved. Her father was getting better, and her mother agreed to let her take up her scholarship and go to high school. Though she was by now two years behind her age cohort, she caught up on what she had missed, became Head Girl, and matriculated with her class. But then she suffered another check. She could not go on to university without a scholarship and, thanks to the Depression, there were almost no scholarships available. Her only alternative seemed to be to get a job, but they were few and far between, and competition was fierce. In *Fence*, she writes that at this time she 'lost hope'.[17] Her ambition of becoming a writer seemed impossible once again: 'unrealistic, a child's romance'. Her parents, who had once indulged her, were now insisting that childhood dreams must be set aside. Her mother was pushing her to become a teacher or a nurse, but for Park, 'The idea of either of these professions, for which I was hideously unfitted temperamentally, gave me cold sweats'.[18] Nevertheless, according to her notes for her autobiography, she did 'a year preparing for Teachers' Training College Entrance, though I had no intention whatsoever of being a teacher. I would have been a factory girl first'.[19] She was ill again, this time with pernicious anaemia. Worst of all, her idol, Elsie Morton, had inexplicably turned on her. Park had sent her yet another story, and Morton had responded with a scrawled note telling her that she would never make it as a writer.

In *Fence*, Park does not linger over this dark period, which ends when she is offered a copyholder's job in the proofreading department of the *Auckland Star*. As a writer, she always kept her reader in mind, and in writing her autobiography her aim was – as she says in her unpublished notes – to ensure the 'pleasure', 'satisfaction', and '(if possible) inspiration' of her audience.[20] But a letter she wrote to her younger sister, Jocelyn, after the publication of *Fence* adds some details. It tells of how, at the age of 'nearly seventeen', she spent almost a year looking for work, at her mother's insistence, standing in queues for hours each day for factory or office jobs, even fainting in the line.[21] (This experience, incidentally, seems to have gone into the depiction of Jackie's job-hunting experiences in Depression-era Sydney in *Swords and Crowns and Rings*.) One day, when she finally made it to an interview, the woman looked her up and down and asked: 'What on earth makes you think that a girl who looks like you would ever get a job?' Park comments:

You can imagine what a remark like that, delivered in
an icy Brit voice did for my self confidence, if indeed I
had any left by that time. It hurt all the more because I
knew how shabby I was, with homecut hair, pimples,
a school uniform [the only decent clothes she had] and
that horrendous grey dirty looking blouse. I suppose
I walked that long way home in a daze of despair,
bleeding from every pore.

She adds that she left 'All of this…out of the first
autobiography, because it was no longer relevant. I came
to terms with it years ago. But I had some rough times.'
Things began to look up when she was offered a job
as a proofreader on the *Auckland Star*. This came about
because of the stories she had published in the children's
pages of both the *Herald* and the *Star*. On the basis of
these stories, she was invited to join 'a little society…
for young people who wanted to write', and through
this society, she met one of her literary heroes, Sheila
Quinn, editor of the *Star*'s children's section.[22] Home-cut
hair and shabby blouse notwithstanding, she impressed
Quinn, who offered her a job. It was the opportunity
Park had despaired of – the 'toe in the door' that was all
she needed. Her lost hopes revived. She would become
a writer after all.

It is at this point that the first cracks begin to appear in
Park's narrative of vocation. Throughout her life until

now, she has wanted nothing more than to become a journalist, and the editor of the children's pages of a big newspaper. This has been synonymous with her dream of being a writer. But when she achieves these ambitions, becoming first a proofreader, then a journalist and finally children's editor at the *Star* – when she at last is able to spend her days writing and getting paid for it – she finds that she is not satisfied. She is a writer, but she is not the writer she wants to be. She is working with 'manic energy' at all kinds of writing jobs – what she calls 'button-sewing...of a literary variety' – but barely making ends meet.[23] And though she has increasing success in placing her stories with other newspapers and journals, she does not have enough time to do the writing she wants to do. To achieve her literary goals, she decides, she will have to leave not only the *Auckland Star* but New Zealand itself.

It is ironic that she decided to come to Australia, where it was generally accepted that, as Geoffrey Serle puts it, 'The only possibility of becoming a serious professional writer was by migrating'.[24] Australia had little to offer a writer in the 1940s and '50s. There were few literary journals and only one serious publisher, Angus & Robertson, which was well known to be cautious and conservative. In addition, rates of pay were low; 'payment for a story in England was five or more times as much as in Australia', according to Serle. And there was little opportunity for 'reviewing, broadcasting, reading for publishers and the other freelance work which normally makes up a large part of a serious writer's earnings'. Yet it was to Sydney that Park came to seek her literary fortune.

It had not been her first choice. She had planned to go to San Francisco, which offered not only larger markets but a haven from the war, which, early in 1941, the United States had not yet joined. She had been offered a job on the *San Francisco Examiner* and was about to sail for America when Japan attacked the US at Pearl Harbor. Suddenly, travelling to San Francisco was no longer an option. Instead, she went to Sydney where, three weeks after her arrival, she married Niland, an impoverished young man with a writing ambition to match her own, with whom she had been corresponding for several years. It was then she began to grapple with the question of whether she should return to journalism or strike out on her own. In the second volume of her autobiography, she says she knocked back the two newspaper jobs she had been offered in Sydney when she saw her first copies of the papers in question: both were tabloids. In any case, though she had enjoyed her time on the *Star* and learned a lot, she knew that journalism was not a stepping stone to the kind of writing life she wanted. At the same time, neither she nor D'Arcy wanted to do anything for a living other than writing.

Their decision to become freelancers was a leap of faith – or, as Park would one day put it, 'a dream for children'.[25] They were desperately poor, having between them no possessions to speak of, no savings, no generous wedding gifts from family and friends, and no possibility of buying a house, or even renting one, as well as being intermittently responsible for D'Arcy's impoverished mother and siblings. They had no buffer, in other words. They had to sell their work or they would be starving and homeless. But they did have some experience of freelancing already and Park, in particular, had developed a good sense of what was involved in writing material that would sell. Even before she left New Zealand, she was giving D'Arcy advice about this by letter. When he complained to Park that editors were treating him badly, she wrote him 'a stinger':

> Use your brains, I shouted. Think first whether the story is appropriate for that journal or paper, whether it's timely, whether the style is right. Don't argue with editors; just ask if they can give you some helpful advice. Who's going to like you when you're pig-headed, obnoxious, and apparently think your head is there to grow hair on?[26]

It's clear that her own knowledge of the literary marketplace, and of how to hawk her wares there, was growing by leaps and bounds. This knowledge was to become the basis of her writing life. In the humorous memoir she and Niland co-wrote in 1955, *The Drums Go Bang*, they state that when they first began freelancing, they were prepared to do any kind of writing at all in order to make a living – and they did. In their first couple of years, they turned their hands not only to their stalwarts of short stories and newspaper articles but also to radio serials, comic skits, sentimental verse, true romance and Westerns, with ghost stories and children's books thrown in for good measure. 'We had a product, and we lived by selling it', they declare. Accordingly, they studied markets, courted editors and learned to please readers: '"Shape it to fit" has to be the freelance motto.'[27]

Both *Drums* and *Fishing in the Styx* paint a picture of back-breaking industry and astounding productivity. Between them, they say, they wrote an average of 60,000 words a month, of which they placed around 15,000.[28] As they saw it, they had no choice. They write in *Drums*:

> We had been told many times we could not make a living from writing alone.... All you could hope to be, we were told, was a hobbyist. But we did not want to be hobbyists. We were in the job because we liked doing it best, and we wanted it to keep us.[29]

It was hard work, they assert, but it was writing. It was their dream life, so it was worth it. 'We worked, early and late, and at everything that came our way', Park writes in *Fishing*:

> We were, in a literary sense, obsessively industrious, partly because we had to work like demons in order to make the most basic of incomes, and mostly because writing was life itself.[30]

Gradually, their strike rate got better. For a long time, they were desperately poor, delivering their manuscripts by hand to save postage, living and working in agonising insecurity, week after week coming down to their last shilling. But they were surviving. Park notes that in their first year of freelancing, 'between us we earned the basic wage for six months…not consistently or consecutively, but on average'.[31] But between writing their 'Bagman' radio ghost stories, a succession of twee verses Niland teasingly referred to as Park's 'Thoughtlets from Thoreau', and the romantic oeuvre of the pseudonymous Ellen Donovan, they did not have much time to meditate on their own masterpieces. At this point, this did not worry them. They were both moulding their writer's identities around the freelancer's creed. In *Fishing*, Park gives their philosophy in Niland's words: the freelancer 'was born to be a writer, not born to be a writer of some specialised type of literature'.[32] They were writing, in other words, and that was enough; what they were writing was not important. In this, they were making a virtue of necessity, as they knew. 'Those who, from the beginning, wrote exactly what they wanted to write', Niland wrote, were possessed of 'a grant, a patron, or a sucker'. Park and Niland, of course, had none of the above.

Park certainly considered herself born to be a writer. But was freelancing the fulfilment of this lifelong desire? Her autobiographies are equivocal on this point. Clearly, neither Park nor Niland was able to write 'exactly what they wanted to write'. But what was it that, if a kindly patron had suddenly blown in, they would have written?

For Niland, the answer was probably stories. In *Fence*, Park writes that Niland's 'ardent desire' was 'to write fine short stories', and his apprenticeship in this was to study and analyse 'most of the great European and American writers'.[33] For Park, however, things were not so clear. She was more successful than D'Arcy at writing for a given market, and more willing and able to diversify, so she did a greater range of work. In fact, in her notes for *Fishing*, she records that she was the main breadwinner for the family, 'though D. worked hard and contributed what he could'.[34] If she had ever had a sense that she wanted to write one particular type of work more than another – novels or children's books, for instance – she does not own it as an adult. As a girl, she wrote nothing but fiction, 'as imaginative as possible'. But in *Fishing*, she says that of all the writing she has done, she has 'most enjoyed writing non-fiction'.[35] A letter she wrote to a student in the mid-1990s revises this, saying that she enjoyed writing for film the most, 'then nonfiction'.[36] She adds: 'I can honestly say that I do my best at any kind of writing. If it doesn't satisfy me, it does not go out.' She is adamant that she is not a novelist. 'I haven't written many novels, something like nine,' she tells Terry O'Connor. 'But then I don't consider myself a novelist, just a person who goes and writes a novel.'[37] She says something similar to William Fraser: 'I didn't think of myself as a novelist. I still don't. I'm a writer – I'll turn my hand to any sort of writing I think I can do well.'[38] Similarly, she tells her student correspondent:

I am not a novelist or children's writer or anything as specific as that. I am a *working writer*, and have written almost everything, and with luck will continue to do so.

What began as a matter of simple necessity – 'I'll turn my hand to any sort of writing' – has become who she is as a writer. There is a moment in *Fishing* when she reflects on this. She is speaking about the career of Jon Cleary, whose first novel came second in the *Sydney Morning Herald* novel competition in 1946, the year that she herself won it with her own first novel, *The Harp in the South*. Unlike Park, Cleary focused his writing efforts after his win on a single genre: novels. 'By turning his face away from the freelance world, he and his family probably had a calmer and more prosperous life than D'Arcy and I had', Park writes. 'But for us novels were only one variety of writing. We were to continue with our richly varied literary endeavours all our lives.'[39] The implication seems to be that though writing novels was a better way to make a living – more secure, more profitable – than freelancing, she and D'Arcy chose not to take that path because they did not want to limit themselves to 'only one variety of writing'. They had adopted their principle of diversification for purely pragmatic reasons, but they continued it, after the publication of Park's bestselling novel, by choice – or so Park claims here. Their output was not just varied but 'richly varied' – variety had become a virtue in itself.

This was probably not strictly true in 1948, when *The Harp in the South* was published. Park is quite clear, in *Fishing*, that despite the seeming windfall of the prize money, the novel did not substantially change their financial situation. They were still living very much from 'typewriter to mouth', as Park puts it.[40] The reason neither had attempted a novel before, she explains, was that they could not afford the time:

> Our meagre circumstances dictated that we write only short material which was quickly paid for. Novels were things we never thought of – so much work, dependent on royalties which might or might not come in. How could we waste time on insubstantial enterprises?[41]

Even when Park had published a handful of successful novels, she and Niland still had to consider carefully whether either could take the risk of writing another. For instance, when D'Arcy's novel *The Big Smoke*, which won second prize in the Commonwealth Jubilee Competition, was knocked back by Angus & Robertson, he wanted to rush straight in and write a new one. But a moment's reflection showed he could not afford this. 'I could write a dozen short stories in the time I'd spend labouring over another clunker', he tells Ruth. She comments that it was true: 'Immediate or near immediate payment was still vital to us.'[42]

Even as a bestselling author, it seems, Park was not in a position to write 'exactly what she wanted to write'.

Increasingly, however, what she wanted to write was what she was writing: anything and everything. The idea of vocation she puts forward here is pragmatic – certainly in comparison with that of other writers. Hewett, for instance, speaks in an interview of 'this terrible sense of urgency that I've got all this great world in my head and I must get it down on paper'. Without pausing for breath, she asks herself why she feels this way. 'Do I think that what I've got to say is so unique and so marvellous that I've got to have the time? Yes, that's part of it, I do think that.'[43] This is typical of the Romantic conception of the artist: what is in me must come out. Even Stead, who had a weather eye out for Romantic pretensions, spoke of the 'urgency' of the creative impulse. The general idea is that writing happens because of a powerful internal imperative, regardless of what is going on in the outside world. It is produced not because there is an audience ready and waiting but, as critic Nettie Palmer once put it, 'because some lonely being has got a live coal inside him'.[44] Park, however, asserts that she writes because she can find buyers for her work.

Nevertheless, her talk of writing for markets, audiences and income – which was unquestionably the reality of her writing life – runs alongside equally persistent descriptions of writing as a kind of truth-telling. In *Fence*, she describes her childhood sense of vocation as 'the feverish desire to grab an instant, a scene, a person, and somehow transmit a concept of these things to other people'.[45] In *Drums*, she and Niland speak in similar terms of their 'joyful and unappeasable hunger to "put it down", to create, however imperfectly, some facsimile of life as we saw it'.[46] In her construction of it, this desire to see and to communicate has a clear moral dimension. As a writer, she has an ethical obligation to depict the world as it is in order to edify – or at least not to mislead – her readers. In *Fence*, she speaks of the need to 'look at your fellows (and yourself, too, by the same token) with total directness', and praises her impoverished upbringing for the painful training it had given her in this.[47] In *Fishing*, she would write of the 'sweaty labour' involved in creating characters who live:

> This is what makes a memorable character, "a real person", as readers often say – motivation deeply and acutely observed by the writer…The world is full of books in which the characters simply *say* and *do*. There are certainly legitimate genres in which this is sufficient. But in real and lasting writing the character *is*.[48]

This idea of creating writing that is 'real and lasting' is perhaps the closest Park comes to an artist's creed. She was born to write 'anything and everything', provided she could make it pay, but her goal was to make that 'anything and everything' live. This did not apply to 'Thoughtlets from Thoreau', perhaps, but it was her aspiration for all her substantial work. Her complex juggling of these two goals – make it real, make it pay – is evident in her account of how she came to write *The Harp in the South*. In both *Drums* and *Fishing*, she is clear that her sole reason for deciding to try her hand at a novel was to enter the *Sydney Morning Herald* prize. Until the prize was announced, she had no thought of any such thing, but the opportunity of the prize money – a lavish £2000 – was too good to pass up. She cast around in her mind for something she could write, something that 'would stretch to eighty thousand words', examining her own experience for anything that might do. Her life in the then-slum area of Surry Hills when she first arrived in Sydney seemed the most promising material, so she sat down to write about that, hoping in the process to 'exorcise the bad memories'.[49]

So far, her creative process as she describes it was entirely pragmatic, the opposite of the Romantic 'spontaneous overflow of powerful feeling'. But once she began to write, she thought not about the *Sydney Morning Herald* judging panel but about her story and her characters. Her primary imperative was to 'tell about these people as if they were real human beings'. She wanted to show 'life, as far as I was capable of depicting it'.[50] In this way, the novel became an expression of herself in the best Romantic sense. In writing it, she sought to draw on her self: her experiences, her perceptions, her sense of life's harsh realities and compensating joys.

This sense that writing is, or should be, an expression of the self, that it is even a kind of amplification of the very process of living, also appears in a handful of letters Park wrote late in life, and helps to make sense of her insistence that she had a vocation to write before she even knew what a writer was. Early in *Fence*, she says that as a child she read and wrote continuously, 'scarcely ever stopping either occupation, as I also read and wrote in my head'.[51] A letter she wrote in 1996 to an aspiring writer gives a clearer sense of what she meant by this. 'True writing', she tells her correspondent, 'is done in the head. It's *you* – thinking or yearning or describing or loving or hating'.[52] In other words, writing is everything a writer is and does, whether it is set down on paper or not. Writing – and even reading, perhaps – is nothing less than the sum total of a writer's being. 'Get that essential woman that you are, that precious individual with her own idiom of thoughts, reactions and passions down on paper,' she urges the aspirant. 'That's what is important.' Moreover, writing is in itself an activity of self-making. 'Even one sentence that is completely *right*, that expresses perfectly what you longed for it to express – even one sentence will strengthen and enrich you.'

Fragments of this view glimmer in other letters. 'Writing is intensely personal, part of the individual psyche', she tells another fan.[53] To yet another correspondent, she declares: 'I realised long ago that a person like myself, who writes about the small corners of life has to go naked, so to speak'.[54] Her words echo those of Sally Banner in *The Chapel Perilous*. Though she would be unlikely to have relished the comparison, Park did have something of Hewett's Romantic sense of the writer's vocation running alongside her determined pragmatism. She was never going to wear a velvet gown and swan around in a mansion entertaining her lovers, but she did share Hewett's sense that writing was as much a state of being – an identity – as it was an activity performed with pen on paper or fingers on keyboard.

Even so, her career as a freelance writer threatened at times to extinguish her writer's identity. It was a constant, and exhausting, dance between two competing imperatives: to meet the needs of the market, on the one hand, and to fulfil her own needs as a writer, on the other. Because earning an income had to be the priority, artistic exploration necessarily took second place. She simply did not have time for the kind of creative play – reading and writing without a specific purpose – that more leisured writers had. As the 'maintenance officer for a reasonably large family', as she describes it, as well as 'an industrious and dedicated writer, not a novelist, not a playwright, not a journalist, but all three', she was always flat out.[55] When she and Niland began freelancing, she was pregnant with their first child, and she would have four more in fairly quick succession. When she discovered, with her fourth pregnancy, that she was having twins, her horrified mother pointed out that she would have 'three babies under a year old!'[56] It would have been a daunting prospect even for someone with access to cheap child care, which was most certainly not available in Sydney in the 1940s. D'Arcy helped out, but it is clear that both he and Ruth took for granted that running the household, doing the cooking, cleaning and washing, and caring for the children were primarily her responsibility. This attitude was very much of its time, of course, and in the 1940s and '50s, they both seem to have played up the idea that Park was a happy housewife combining writing with cheerful domesticity. A *Sunday Herald* column from 1949 by 'Jack Meander' is a case in point. Meander says that he rang Niland to congratulate him on his wins in a recent *Herald* literary competition. 'Happy as Hemingway, Mr. Niland was still in bed', he writes. 'While I was on the phone, he called out for his wife to bring in his breakfast. Mrs. Niland put down the phone and obediently took in Mr. Niland's breakfast.' He adds, with evident enjoyment, that 'Besides being a good cook, Mrs. Niland has written a couple of prize-winning novels herself being, of course, Ruth Park.'[57]

The image of the literary prize–winning Park as an 'obedient' housewife rushing to serve her husband breakfast in bed defuses any threat to masculine dominance her success might otherwise have posed. Perhaps this is why she colluded in this image of herself as a housewife-who-writes, as opposed to a writer-who-keeps-house. In a newspaper article she wrote in the same year, she depicted herself shelling peas as she worked through ideas for a story, 'burn[ing] saucepans between sentences', 'tear[ing] off' in the midst of writing a powerful scene 'to poke the clothes down in the copper'.[58] She made a lighthearted story out of her domestic work, as she did in *Drums* – fully aware that this would sell. And there is no doubt she did not begrudge her labour, and very much wanted to be at home with her children. Being able to do that was for her one of the great benefits of freelancing. Yet it took its toll. In *Fishing*, she describes a dark time when, with all five of her children down with chickenpox and D'Arcy away, she found herself questioning everything she had dedicated her life to. 'I experienced a terrible feeling of futility', she writes.

For what was it all about? It seemed that from my earliest years I had been running, always catching up on something – often breathless, often with a stitch in my side. It was true I had had, as the world saw it, considerable success. Yet, was the struggle worth it?... After so many years of hard running, I acknowledged I did not get from my life much that was satisfying.[59]

Her own explanation of this 'disquieting and deeply melancholy feeling' was that she was burnt out. (She also considers a spiritual explanation, pondering whether her feeling was simply an expression of her 'entrapment...in the vast religious and ethical error of constructiveness', the belief that life must necessarily be heading somewhere, rather than simply happening.) Though she pushed it down, her disquiet did not go away. Later, as she 'managed a large household, listened to children's woes and joys, wrote scripts for the [ABC Radio's] *Children's Session*, and finished a novel that required much historical research in a poorly documented period', she found herself darkly convinced that 'things could only get more complex, more burdensome, less rewarding for me'. She was suffering from 'unstructured discontent', a 'feeling that I was not only in a trap with no way out, but that I didn't know why I was in a trap'.[60]

This moment marks a kind of rupture in the text. Up until this point, Park had been adamant that writing was the purpose of her life, the only way she could consider spending her time, her driving compulsion, her contribution to the world. Furthermore, she had insisted that the busy, crazy, challenging and enchanting life of the freelance writer was the ideal way for her to live out her writing vocation. She and Niland had made for themselves, against the odds, the very life they most wanted: one in which they were respected as writers, and able to support themselves and their family by doing what they loved. According to the logic of her narrative – a struggle against almost insuperable barriers to achieve her dream – she should have been blissfully happy. Instead, she suddenly felt the need for 'another dimension'.[61] When D'Arcy had a near-fatal heart attack, her discontent became urgent. D'Arcy's own view was that, with their children and a house of their own at last, they did indeed have everything they needed. But when he asked her what more she could want, she was ready with her answer: 'Life for ourselves, leisure to think. Study. Travel.'[62]

For the first time in her text, she distinguishes her life goals from Niland's. Up until this point, she had depicted the two of them as entirely united in and by their devotion to writing. In the first year of their marriage, she writes, she was 'electric with energy... because for the first time in my life I was living intimately with someone whose entire psyche was directed towards writing and the study of writing'.[63] She was always clear that this shared passion was the basis of their marriage. 'Writing was and is the great love of my life, as it was for D'Arcy Niland', she wrote in a 1994 letter. 'This was the reason we had a great time together, and achieved a mutual literary growth'.[64] Yet, suddenly, she and D'Arcy were no longer united in their devotion. 'Writing was his mainspring', she writes in *Fishing*. 'Time spent at the typewriter was time spent doing exactly what he was born for. But I was born for many other things'.[65]

This separation of herself from D'Arcy, of her goals from his, also marks a separation in herself. From her earliest years, she had seen the writer within as her 'true self'; her task was to take this hidden reality and make it manifest in her life. Yet somehow, in the process of doing this, her writing self – the hard-working, highly respected professional writer – had come adrift from her 'true' self. This, at least, is what a slightly slant reading of her autobiography would suggest. Early in *Fishing*, she writes that as a freelancer, she had had to learn 'not to allow emotion to interfere with the pursuit of writing'.[66] Whatever crises were going on in her life, she had to be able to sit down and write her story or radio episode or newspaper article just as though nothing was wrong. If she didn't, they would not be able to pay their bills. It was a skill that enabled her to survive financially after D'Arcy's untimely death. 'A lifetime of literary practice had taught me that I no longer had to know delight, or humour, or energy in order to convey it', she writes. 'The woman and the writer were separate'.[67]

But though this is clearly a necessary skill for a

freelancer, it carried with it for Park the risk that the process of writing would become meaningless. Park's whole philosophy – and the source of the power of her literary vocation – was that the woman and the writer were the same: the one was the expression of the other. If they were separated, writing would lose its purpose. This does not mean that the quality of the writing would suffer, necessarily; Park's whole point was that she could write well under any circumstances. But the internal motivation for that writing, its source deep in her own self, would be gone, and so the writing itself might well come to seem futile. Park seems to have experienced something like this in midlife.

Nevertheless, the overarching narrative of her auto-biography – that she was meant to be a writer, and would always be a writer – remains in place. Moreover, the calm confidence, the sheer writerly accomplishment of these two volumes, bears witness to this underlying truth. Yet the brief writing journal Park kept when she was working on *Fishing* paints a very different picture of her daily experience as a writer, documenting anxiety, uncertainty and doubt. She ends one early entry, for example, with her determination to get down to work on 'that first paragraph, which I am determined to find this morning', and begins the next with a lament that 'I have not succeeded in writing a usable sentence'.[68] At times she despairs of what she has done. 'I suppose I was tackling the problem the wrong way as usual', she writes of one early draft. 'But one can only learn one is wrong by trying over and over again. Such labour it is.' Elsewhere, she speaks of 'panic', 'frustration' and 'despair', and indeed the journal ends abruptly on a dark note: 'I simply do not know where to go from here'. Written for herself and not for a reader, this brief record of her writing experience suggests that doubt was very much the condition of her vocation – along with the certainty that kept her returning to her desk.

The question I've been skirting is whether Park might have written differently if she had had more time and less financial pressure. Did her commercial focus get in the way of her pursuit of artistic goals? It is a question I am sure Park herself would have dismissed out of hand, at least in these terms. She did not see herself as having 'artistic goals' but only as wanting – needing – to write. Yet at the end of *Fishing*, pondering the 'puzzle of writing, a passion I have never understood', she steers close to this dangerous territory. 'What had I always wanted to write?' she asks herself. 'What kind of thing?'[69] After a lifetime of writing, she is not sure of the answer. This is, I think, because when she became a freelancer, she ceased to ask the question. She ceased to consult her own preference and focused on what would sell. This does not mean that she did not put herself into her work, or that she produced work she was not proud of. It only means that the initial creative impetus for each project came not from her own urgent need to say some particular thing – to borrow a phrase from Stead – but from the opportunities that arose in the literary marketplace.

This is not necessarily a bad thing. She did not have to suffer the agonising bafflement, described by many an aspiring writer, of staring endlessly at the blank page waiting for her incomprehensibly reluctant soul to rise up and express itself. She had a compelling reason to find the words, and find the words she did. If she had been able to spend ten years crafting each novel, would she have written episode after episode of *The Muddle-Headed Wombat* – surely one of the most beloved creations in Australian fiction? Would she have written such gems of children's literature as *Callie's Castle* and *Playing Beatie Bow*? Would she have contemplated writing a book like *The Harp in the South* if she had not urgently needed money? Despite its bestseller status, *The Harp* is probably the work considered Park's most 'literary'. It has been on the high school curriculum for many years, and constitutes a shared literary–cultural experience for a generation of Australians. It has often been remarked that by making Sydney into fiction, Park made her city real. A quick survey of *Sydney Morning Herald* articles over the past fifteen years shows that it's virtually impossible for a journalist to write about Surry Hills without mentioning *The Harp*. It's no exaggeration to say that this book changed the way Australians saw themselves. Before its publication, there were many who denied there were slums in Sydney, but its impact went beyond this (largely unwelcome) revelation. As Marion Halligan puts it, 'There was something about the urban landscape that Ruth Park helped us start seeing'.[70]

All of this she did with one eye fixed on sales – and without compromising her own standards. Critical opinion on Park has long been divided. Reviewing *A Fence Around the Cuckoo* in the *Sydney Morning Herald* in 1992, Andrew Riemer calls her 'a true artist', while a decade later, Alex Buzo praises the 'beautiful, poetic quality to her writing' in *Sydney*, her guidebook to the city she loved.[71] Yet the editors of 2009's *Macquarie PEN Anthology of Australian Literature* declined to include any of Park's work, and Susan Wyndham reported in the *Sydney Morning Herald* that Park had been rejected on the grounds that her novels had been written 'for a popular audience of a particular time' and 'did not look good among the other works'.[72]

Park herself claimed to be indifferent to the critics, responding to a student's declaration that the academy had largely ignored her by quipping: 'To think that my whole life I have thought the situation the other way round!'[73] She did not consider herself a literary writer, and had little patience for what she saw as artistic pretension. Yet it seems clear that if she had only had more time, and the opportunities for education, travel and reflection that, as Woolf points out, have so often been denied women, she may well have been as literary – indeed, as pretentious, in her own terms – as Harwood, Hewett and Stead. Her childhood sense of her writer's identity was like theirs, but as a working-class girl, she had neither the leisure nor the chutzpah to claim an identity as an artist.

In the second half of her life, she did find ways to pursue those 'other dimensions' she had so often felt to be missing. She and Niland went overseas together, as she had longed to do, and after his death she continued to travel. Eventually, she gained that precious 'time to think' when her children were all grown and she was no longer financially responsible for them. Even then, though, she did not have the kind of financial freedom she had fought for all her life. Only a government grant to write a novel made it financially viable for her to take time off from her freelance schedule and move to Norfolk Island. In her description of this time in *Fishing*, she makes it sound as though writing the novel was secondary: her main goal was to have some time alone so that she could finally come to terms with her grief over D'Arcy's death. The novel was one that had been 'floating around in the back of my head' for years, 'a story about a dwarf and his attitudes towards a world monstrous in its dimensions, but never too big for him'.[74] The story became *Swords and Crowns and Rings*, and won the Miles Franklin Award in 1977.

Park continued, however, to see herself as a freelancer, a working writer who could turn her hand to almost anything. If there had ever been a time when she wanted to write one thing more than another, it was past. She declares at the end of *Fishing*:

All I wanted was to write stories, short or long, fact or fiction, in which the reader could walk about, see a familiar reflection in the looking-glass, say, 'Oh, yes, I know! I've been here all the time but didn't realise it.'[75]

The life of a freelance writer was one she adopted out of necessity, both psychological and financial, but it became who she was. It became the means by which – in her own mind, at least – she fulfilled her vocation. If it was also the source of a disconcerting late rupture in her identity, this was something she could live with.

Epilogue

While working on this book, I began to see intimations of vocation everywhere. Almost everything I read, no matter how random, seemed to offer some insight. One of the most unexpected was a passage I came across in Mervyn Peake's dark and strange fantasy, *Titus Groan*, from which I drew my title. The narrator is describing Fuchsia, the young daughter of Lord Groan, and the secret attics she has made her own. These attics are full of fascinating rubbish from past ages of the ancient castle and precious detritus from her own life, and they form her theatre of 'make-believe', where she invents scenes and plots and characters and imagines them playing out. As she steps into the hidden stairwell, her heart begins to pound with her passion for this secret place. What she feels is akin to intense sexual love, the narrator tells us, yet it is not sex that makes Fuchsia tremble. Rather, it is love for the thing at the centre of her self and her world, the one place where her life burns 'genuinely and with a free flame'.

This is the concept of vocation at its most romantic: vocation as the site of our most perfect self. In fact, Peake goes on to make the analogy clear. What Fuchsia feels, he says, is what the diver feels, what the painter feels, what the farmer feels as they go to the place where their work is done. 'As the pearl diver murmurs, "I am home" as he moves dimly in strange water-lights, and as the painter mutters, "I am me" on his lone raft of floorboards, so the slow landsman on his acre'd marl.' All are in love. All say, 'with dark Fuchsia on her twisting staircase, "I am home"'.[1]

There is something infinitely seductive in the idea of vocation as the place where one's life 'burns genuinely and with a free flame'. Vocation becomes the ultimate in self-realisation, the place where the inner self and the outer world meet, a wild adventure that is also one's final refuge. This is the ideal evident in Harwood, Hewett, Stead and Park's conceptions of their identity as writers. Yet they never seem quite to reach that place. In their own tellings, their stories are quest narratives in which the perfect fulfilment of their writing ambitions is the Holy Grail; as in all such stories, the Grail remains just out of reach. For each woman, every step on the path to living the life of the writer she knew herself to be ushered in a new set of struggles. But this, too, is part of the myth of vocation: one of the marks of the true artist is the lifelong struggle to survive and triumph. Thus, even in their depictions of their difficulties and setbacks, it's not difficult to see the underlying narrative of vocation guiding their stories. In *Fishing in the Styx*, for instance, Park quotes Flaubert on the dubious joys of writing:

> When I find I haven't written a single sentence of worth after scribbling dozens of pages I collapse on my couch and lie there dazed, bogged in a swamp of despair, hating myself. O, if you knew the torture I suffer![2]

Flaubert's experience validates her own: it is part of the quintessential writer's journey.

Stead, too, was known to complain about the long hours she spent at the typewriter, and the agonising labour of rewriting and revising. She speaks of insomnia, heart palpitations and long periods of heavy misery. Writing *The Man Who Loved Children*, she says, was a torment: 'I tore it out of me alive and I can still remember those awful feelings.'[3] Dorothy Hewett depicts her struggles in similar terms. Working on *The Chapel Perilous*, she told an interviewer, 'nearly killed me':

> It took me much longer than anything I'd ever written, I worked over and over it a thousand times, particularly the second act. It nearly drove me mad. I couldn't sleep, I couldn't do anything, I was just obsessed with this play which was like some terrible twin birth which wouldn't be born.[4]

Such depictions of struggle, however, only serve to emphasise the truly creative nature of their work — and the extent to which it was an expression of themselves, a very child of their bodies, born in suffering and blood, and not a 'consumable', hygienically produced according to marketplace requirements. Their struggles to create were luxurious ones, epic battles which showed the aspirant's strength and worthiness.

Less consonant with the myth, however, are experiences of doubt about the truth of one's vocation. The basis of vocation is the sense of calling; to doubt that is to doubt everything, to challenge the very foundations on which one has built one's life. Yet all four women had such moments of doubt, times when they feared that the sense of vocation they had put at the centre of their identity was mere self-delusion. In the holiest myth of the artist, the writer is an exalted being. As a young Miles Franklin put it in the preface to her first novel, *My Brilliant Career*, the soul of the artist is 'as far above common mortals as common mortals are above monkeys'. But if artists were transcendent creatures, women were the earthiest of all earthy beings. As Drusilla Modjeska and others have pointed out, women's social and cultural status has traditionally been low, creating a 'fundamental contradiction' between the cultural value accorded to the writer and that allotted to the woman.[5] Inevitably, this was internalised. All the women in this book had moments when they asked themselves – to borrow the words of a young Janet Frame – 'Who did I think I was, to imagine I'd be a poet?'[6] The question was unanswerable, except by clinging to a fragile faith that the 'gift' of vocation could be given to anyone, regardless of gender.

For all four women, their moments of doubt were fuelled by rejections of their work. Harwood felt so discouraged when she first began trying to publish that she spoke repeatedly in letters of giving up. Both Stead and Hewett had the depressing experience of discovering that even as well-established writers, they would still find it difficult to persuade publishers to take them on. After the publication of her ninth book, *The People with the Dogs*, in 1952, Stead did not publish another book for thirteen years, though she finished three novels in that time and worked endlessly on a fourth. No publisher would take her work, despite the fact that her earlier novels had all won a degree of critical acclaim, and some had sold well. Publishers were simply not interested in taking a risk with work one publisher's reader characterised as 'strange, and commercially difficult'.[7] Stead found this profoundly disheartening. She knew she did not have what she called 'the moneymaking style', but she did expect to be able to make 'a mediocre living' from her books. She was to discover that, as she wrote to her cousin Gwen, literature was 'another word for slow-starvation'.[8]

Park, too, struggled both with numerous rejections – though only in the early stages of her career – and real poverty, and her autobiography includes accounts of several moments where she 'gave up'. Hewett also gave up more than once as a young woman, and speaks of times when she vowed to stop writing in response to intense negative criticism. She told an interviewer that she felt she was 'criticised in ways which were very personal and hurtful', citing a female journalist's description of her as 'a varicosed

Barbie doll'.[9] When her play *Pandora's Cross,* performed in Sydney in 1978, was savaged by critics, it closed after just two weeks. The experience was 'shattering' for Hewett, who decided she 'wouldn't write for theatre again, it was just too painful'.[10] But even this experience could not lead her permanently to abandon what she believed to be her calling, and she did return to writing plays.

External attacks could be debilitating, but internal doubts were the most potent enemy. No matter what was happening in terms of publications, reviews, critics and sales, each writer had her own internal dialogue about whether her work was of true value, whether what she was writing mattered, whether she was any good. 'You are wrong in imagining that I don't doubt my own talent', Harwood wrote to a friend in 1958:

> I am continually in doubt about what I write, especially as I reflect that if people don't like what I've done already (and on the whole they DON'T) I might as well clean the windows.[11]

Years later, in her poem 'To A. D. Hope', she would speak of how she and Hope shared the same fear: that for all their high aspirations, they were mere hacks, the twentieth-century equivalent of laughable nineteenth-century poets like Martin Tupper and Eliza Cook, who were the butts of many a Harwood joke. The 'bardic robes assumed ideally / right might be tattered,' she writes. Like Hope, she grappled 'through the same / night-watches with self-doubt'.

Hewett, too, once admitted in an interview that she was 'terribly worried' about her standing after her death. 'If you don't think you'll ever make it when you're alive you better bloody make it when you're dead', she says.[12] As a girl, she had looked up at the names of famous women 'engraved in gold letters' around her school hall and known 'with absolute certainty' that her name would one day be among them.[13] As an established writer, she feared that history would judge her to be – like Sally in *The Chapel Perilous* – merely 'a minor poet'. Her own feeling was that she never quite succeeded in any of her works: 'I'm never satisfied with anything I do. I always feel a terrible sense of failure at the end.'[14]

Park's view of herself was that she was not a 'great' writer. 'Thank God I know, have always known, too much about writing ever to think I was great', she told an interviewer. 'I thought with experience and practice I could be a competent writer. This is all I have ever felt about it.'[15] This is not to say that she did not take pride in her writing, and particularly in her professionalism, and the extraordinary range of genres in which she had written outstandingly well. But she made no large claims for herself beyond the assertion that writing was her calling. Even Stead, who seems never to have shied away from large claims, felt that her published works did not live up to her hopes for them. In a letter she wrote when she was in her late sixties, for instance, she said that she had hated writing her masterpiece, *The Man Who Loved Children*: 'Bill had to tear [it] out of my hands – because I felt it was so bad, unfinished.'[16] Even with her other books, she did not feel 'exactly satisfied' when she had finished them. 'When I yield a book up I feel, "Well, I've pushed that as far as I can…No more can be done with this poor cripple."'

It is not exactly a glowing account of ecstatically fulfilled creativity. All of these women felt absolutely driven to spend their lives writing, and overcame daunting obstacles to do so, yet their sense of vocation did not translate into any kind of certainty about their writing careers. Nor was it any guarantee of success, either artistically or commercially. What it did give them, however, was an extraordinary, almost incredible, persistence. It enabled them to keep going when logic and feeling and even sheer survival seemed against it. The belief that they were doing what they were supposed to be doing gave their lives an overarching purpose that meant that no discouragement or obstacle could deter them for long. Such persistence is necessary for all writers, but is especially important for women – indeed, for anyone who does not fit the traditional image of the artist in the West, whether they are female or 'colonial' or poor, uneducated or of any descent other than European, housewives or secretaries or academics, mothers or vamps or victims. For this reason alone, the conviction that you are 'meant' to be a writer is an incredibly powerful thing, wherever the conviction springs from. It is not a sufficient condition, perhaps, to make you a writer, in a world in which that title is bestowed according to complex configurations of markets and media, but it is surely a necessary one. So, at least, these women's stories would suggest.

Notes

Demon Lover: Gwen Harwood

All Harwood poems cited in this chapter are from A. Hoddinott & G. Kratzmann (eds.), *Gwen Harwood Collected Poems: 1943–1995*, University of Queensland Press, Brisbane, 2003.

1 Letter to A. Hoddinott, 28 February 1990, UQFL332, Box 3, Folder 15, Fryer Library, University of Queensland Library.
2 A. Hoddinott (ed.), *Blessed City: Letters to Thomas Riddell 1943*, Collins/Angus & Robertson, Sydney, 1990, p. 146.
3 ibid., p. 109.
4 ibid., p. 289.
5 ibid., p. 257.
6 'Combined recital: pianists and elocutionists', *The Courier Mail*, 7 December 1936, p. 20.
7 'Promising young pianist: Mr. Rubinstein impressed', *Courier Mail*, 18 October 1937, p. 17.
8 'Solo pianist', *The Telegraph* (Brisbane), 1 May 1940, p. 14; 'Fine Music, Elocution At Prize-giving', *Courier Mail*, 18 May 1940, p. 17.
9 G. Harwood, 'Time Beyond Reason', in Robert Sellick (ed.), *Gwen Harwood*, CRNLE Essays & Monographs Series No. 3, Centre for Research in the New Literatures in English, Adelaide, 1987, p. 16.
10 *Gwen Harwood*, video recording, The Writers: Archival Film Series, Australia Council, Sydney, 1987.
11 A. Bennett, *Our Women*, George H. Doran, New York, 1920, p. 113.
12 J. Digby, *A Woman's Voice: Conversations with Australian Poets*, University of Queensland Press, St Lucia, 1996, p. 46.

13 C. Korsmeyer, *Gender and Aesthetics: An Introduction*, Routledge, New York, 2004.

14 Letter to Vincent Buckley, 20 November 1961, National Library of Australia (MS7289/1/1).

15 G. Kratzmann (ed.), *A Steady Storm of Correspondence: Selected Letters of Gwen Harwood 1943–1995*, University of Queensland Press, Brisbane, 2001, pp. 73–4.

16 Letter to Vincent Buckley, 20 November 1961.

17 Digby, *A Woman's Voice*, p. 46.

18 G. Harwood, 'Memoirs of a Dutiful Librettist', in Robert Sellick (ed.), *Gwen Harwood*, CRNLE Essays & Monographs Series No. 3, Centre for Research in the New Literatures in English, Adelaide, 1987, p. 4.

19 Harwood, 'Time Beyond Reason', p. 20.

20 'The Waldstein', in Hoddinott & Kratzmann, *Collected Poems*, p. 44.

21 Letter to Tony Riddell, 12 April 1959, UQFL45, Box 7, Folder 12; origin of quote unknown.

22 Kratzmann, *Steady Storm*, p. 159.

23 ibid., p. 65.

24 'Syntax of the Mind', ibid., p. 456.

25 Anne Boyd cites Margaret Fuller's *Woman in the Nineteenth Century*, published in 1845, to show that Transcendentalism encouraged women to 'shun society's definitions of who they should be and look inward to discover their "true" natures'. By telling them that they were 'beholden only to God', it enabled them to discard social, religious or familial roles and expectations and work out for themselves who they were. A. E. Boyd, *Writing for Immortality: Women and the Emergence of High Literary Culture in America*, Johns Hopkins University Press, Baltimore, 2004, p. 21.

26 V. Woolf, *A Room of One's Own/Three Guineas*, Penguin, London, 1993, p. 34.

27 Letter to Edwin Tanner, 5 September 1961, UQFL45, Box 6, Folder 21.

28 Kratzmann, *Steady Storm*, pp. 44, 48 & 47.

29 ibid., p. 249.

30 B. Williams, 'Interview with Gwen Harwood', *Westerly*, vol. 33, no. 4, 1988, p. 57.

31 Kratzmann, *Steady Storm*, p. 92.

32 Letter to Edwin Tanner, 21 August 1962, UQFL45, Box 6, Folder 21.

33 Letter to Edwin Tanner, Undated, UQFL45, Box 6, Folder 21.

34 Letter to Edwin Tanner, 20 February 1961, UQFL45, Box 6, Folder 21.

35 Letter to Edwin Tanner, 27 April 1971, UQFL45, Box 6, Folder 21.

36 Williams, 'Interview', p. 54.

37 Letter to Edwin Tanner,13 April 1973, UQFL45, Box 6, Folder 21.

38 'Little Buttercup's Picture Book', Hoddinott & Kratzmann, *Collected Poems*, pp. 447–8.

39 Letter to Edwin Tanner, 13 April 1973.

40 G. Harwood, 'Lamplit Presences', *Southerly*, vol. 40, no. 3, 1980, p. 254.

41 'Night Thoughts: Baby and Demon', Hoddinott & Kratzmann, *Collected Poems*, p. 267.

42 Kratzmann, *Steady Storm*, p. 421.

43 ibid., p. 405.

44 ibid., p. 392.

45 ibid., pp. 421 & 393.

46 'Herongate', Hoddinott & Kratzmann, *Collected Poems*, p. 481.

47 Kratzmann, *Steady Storm*, p. 421.

48 ibid., p. 422.

49 E. Showalter, *A Literature of Their Own: British Women Novelists from Bronte to Lessing*, Princeton University Press, Princeton, 1977, p. 68.

50 ibid., p. 68.

51 Gerald Massey, cited in ibid., p. 76.

52 C. Stead, *The Man Who Loved Children*, Penguin, Harmondsworth, Middlesex, 1970, p. 143.

53 'Later Texts I', Hoddinott & Kratzmann, *Collected Poems*, p. 487.

54 '"It was an accident/the milk was spilt"', ibid., p. 538.

The Dark Tower: Dorothy Hewett

1 'Lines to the Dark Tower', in D. Hewett, *Peninsula*, Fremantle Arts Centre Press, South Fremantle, 1994, p. 32.

2 H. De Berg, *Dorothy Hewett interviewed by Hazel De Berg*, sound recording, Hazel de Berg collection, National Library of Australia, Canberra, 11 March 1973.

3 A. Tennyson, *Poetical Works of Alfred Lord Tennyson*, Macmillan, London, 1908, p. 29.

4 Notebook, c.1939–1940, National Library of Australia (MS6184/5).

5 De Berg, *Dorothy Hewett*.

6 D. Hewett, *Wild Card: An Autobiography 1923–1958*, Penguin, Ringwood, 2001, p. 35.

7 De Berg, *Dorothy Hewett*.

8 The Hand that Rocks the Cradle Rules the World [essay in school exercise book], 1939/1940, National Library of Australia (MS6184/5).

9 Hewett, *Wild Card*, p. 25.

10 J. Davidson, *Dorothy Hewett interviewed by Jim Davidson in Meanjin Collection*, sound recording, ORAL TRC 5217/9, National Library of Australia, Canberra, 1979.

11 Hewett, *Wild Card*, p. 86.

12 ibid., p. 88.

13 De Berg, *Dorothy Hewett*.

14 Hewett, *Wild Card*, p. 19.

15 De Berg, *Dorothy Hewett*.

16 Hewett, *Wild Card*, p. 90.

17 ibid.

18 ibid., p. 91.

19 D. H. Lawrence to Ernest Collings, 17 January 1913, in *The Selected Letters of D. H. Lawrence*, Cambridge University Press, Cambridge, 2000, p. 53; D. Hewett, *The Chapel Perilous, or the Perilous Adventures of Sally Banner* (1972), 3rd edn, Currency Press, Sydney, 1981, p. 29.

20 Hewett, *Wild Card*, pp. 14, 15 & 17.

21 ibid., p. 11.

22 'Sex on the Farm', in *Halfway up the Mountain*, Fremantle Arts Centre Press, Fremantle, 2001, p. 81.

23 Hewett, *Wild Card*, p. 74.

24 ibid., pp. 91, 92 & 93.

25 ibid., p. 81.

26 ibid.

27 ibid., p. 104.

28 ibid., p. 83.

29 ibid., p. 104.

30 Joanna Russ, for example, comments on the persistence of 'the assumption that acting, when women did it, was tantamount to prostitution', and cites English theatre critic Clement Scott's notorious remark from the late 1890s that 'actresses are not, as a rule . . . "pure," and their prospects frequently depend on the nature and extent of their compliances': J. Russ, *How to Suppress Women's Writing*, The Women's Press, London, 1983, p. 26.

31 Hewett, *Wild Card*, p. 97.

32 ibid., p. 119.

33 Hewett, *Chapel Perilous*, pp. 24, 28, 29, 33, 42, 68, 24 & 35.

34 Hewett, *Wild Card*, p. 107.

35 ibid., p. 105.

36 ibid., p. 111.

37 Davidson, *Dorothy Hewett*; cf. Baker: 'I really wasn't handling my life at all well': C. Baker, *Yacker: Australian Writers Talk About Their Work*, Picador, Sydney, 1986, pp. 190–1.

38 Hewett, *Chapel Perilous*, p. 55.

39 Hewett, *Wild Card*, p. 174.

40 D. Modjeska, 'Dorothy Hewett talking with Drusilla Modjeska', in M. Chamberlain (ed.), *Writing Lives: Conversations between Women Writers*, Virago, London, 1988, p. 93.

41 Showalter, *A Literature of Their Own*, p. 22.

42 S. Bowen, *Drawn from Life: A Memoir* (1941), Pan Macmillan, Sydney, 1999, p. 224.

43 E. Spires, 'The art of poetry No. 27: Elizabeth Bishop', *The Paris Review*, vol. 23, 1981, p. 79.

44 Hewett, *Wild Card*, p. 122.

45 ibid., p. 111.

46 ibid., p. 119.

47 De Berg, *Dorothy Hewett*.

48 J. Tranter, 'Dorothy Hewett interviewed by John Tranter for Radio Helicon (ABC) broadcast 13 May 1987', *Southerly,* vol. 63, no. 2, 2003, p. 14.

49 N. Moore, 'Jill-of-All-Trades', *Overland,* vol. 153, 1998, p. 37.

50 Hewett, *Wild Card*, p. 152.

51 De Berg, *Dorothy Hewett.*

52 Tranter, *Southerly*, p. 14.

53 Moore, *Overland*, p. 36.

54 Digby, *A Woman's Voice*, p. 232.

55 De Berg, *Dorothy Hewett.*

56 ibid.

57 'Poem 53', *Alice in Wormland*, Paper Bark Press, Paddington, NSW, 1987, p. 112.

58 'Poem 58', ibid., p. 120.

59 'Poem 60', ibid., p. 123.

60 'Poem 63', ibid., pp. 127–8.

61 Hewett, *Wild Card*, p. 87.

62 'Poem 61', *Alice in Wormland*, p. 124.

63 *The Toucher*, McPhee Gribble, Ringwood, 1993, p. 266.

64 ibid., p. 267.

65 'Poem 33', *Alice in Wormland,* p. 59.

66 'Winter in Sydney', *Peninsula*, p. 108.

67 Davidson, *Dorothy Hewett.*

68 'Poem 54', *Alice in Wormland*, p. 113.

69 'Writing Poems in the Blue Mountains', *Halfway*, p. 44.

70 'Writing Poems', ibid., p. 47.

71 'Conversations', *Rapunzel*, p. 58.

72 'In the Garden', *Peninsula*, p. 131.

73 'The Prawn Bird', *Halfway*, p. 129.

A Rebel and a Wanderer: Christina Stead

1 C. Stead, *The Man Who Loved Children*, Penguin, Harmondsworth, Middlesex, 1970, p. 86.

2 C. Stead, *A Web of Friendship: Selected Letters (1928–1973)*, R.G. Geering (ed.), Angus & Robertson, Pymble, 1992.

3   R. Drewe, 'Christina Stead: Interview', in C. Baker (ed.), *Yacker: Australian Writers Talk About Their Work*, Picador, Sydney, 1986, p. 20.

4   J. Lidoff, *Christina Stead*, Frederick Ungur Publishing, New York, 1982, pp. 190 & 201.

5   Stead, *Web*, p. 80.

6   C. Stead, *For Love Alone*, Angus & Robertson, London, 1979, p 82.

7   Lidoff, *Christina Stead*, p. 188.

8   Stead, *For Love Alone*, pp. 136 & 137.

9   H. Rowley, *Christina Stead: A Biography*, Minerva, Port Melbourne, 1994, pp. 56–7.

10 C. Stead & W. J. Blake, *Dearest Munx: The Letters of Christina Stead and William J. Blake*, Margaret Harris (ed.), The Miegunyah Press, Carlton, 2005, p. 224.

11 Stead, *Web*, pp. 61–2.

12 Lidoff, *Christina Stead*, p. 183; A. Chisholm, 'Stead', Interview with Christina Stead, *National Times*, 29 March – 4 April 1981, p. 32; Drewe, 'Christina Stead: Interview', pp. 20 & 22.

13 Drewe, 'Christina Stead: Interview', p. 22; B. Hill, 'Christina Stead at 80 Says Love Is Her Religion: Interview', *Sydney Morning Herald*, 17 July 1982, p. 33; G. Giuffré, *A Writing Life: Interviews with Australian Women Writers*, Allen & Unwin, Sydney, 1990, p. 74.

14 As Rowley points out, Stead was courted before she left Sydney by Colin Lawson, a salesman at the hat factory at which she worked: *Christina Stead*, p. 65.

15 Cited in Rowley, *Christina Stead*, p. 15.

16 Cited in C. Williams, *Christina Stead: A Life of Letters*, McPhee Gribble, Melbourne, 1989, pp. 310–11.

17 For instance, R. Wetherell, 'Interview with Christina Stead', *Australian Literary Studies*, vol. 9, no. 4, 1980, p. 437.

18 R. Jarrell, 'An Unread Book', introduction, C. Stead, *The Man Who Loved Children*, Harmondsworth, Middlesex, Penguin, 1970, p. 14.

19 Lidoff, *Christina Stead*, p. 184.

20 Rowley, *Christina Stead*, p. 260.

21 ibid., p. 20.

22 H. Stewart, 'Feminism and Male Chauvinism in the Writings of Christina Stead (1902–1983)', *Hecate*, vol. 29, no. 2, 2003, p. 117.

23 C. Stead, *Talking into the Typewriter: Selected Letters (1973–1983)*, R. G. Geering (ed.), Angus & Robertson, Pymble, 1992, p. 370.

24 Stead, *Man*, p. 340.

25 ibid., pp. 98–9.

26 ibid., p. 149.

27 ibid., pp. 410–11.

28 ibid., p. 442.

29 ibid., p. 480.

30 ibid., p. 146.

31 Stead, *Talking*, p. 120.

32 Stead, *For Love Alone,* p. 14.

33 For example, Wetherell, *Australian Literary Studies*, p. 437; Lidoff, *Christina Stead*, p. 213.

34 B. L. Baer, 'Rereading Christina Stead', Letter to the Editor, Book Review Desk, *The New York Times*, 27 June 2010, p. 5.

35 Cited in Stewart, 'Feminism', pp. 119–20.

36 Wetherell, *Australian Literary Studies*, p. 447.

37 A. Whitehead, 'Interview with Christina Stead', *Australian Literary Studies*, vol. 6, no. 3, 1974, p. 235.

38 Lidoff, *Christina Stead*, p. 197.

39 Stead, *Web*, p. 90.

40 Stead, *Man*, p. 440.

41 Stead & Blake, *Dearest Munx*, p. 201.

42 Rowley, *Christina Stead*, p. 53.

43 Stewart, 'Feminism', p. 119.

44 Cited in Williams, *Christina Stead*, p. 146.

45 Letter to Edith Anderson, 14 November 1950, National Library of Australia (MS9404-9405).

46 Stead, *Web*, pp. 296 & 297.

47 Letter to Edith Anderson, 12 June 1962, National Library of Australia (MS9404-9405).

48 Stewart, 'Feminism', p. 120.

49 *Christina Stead*, video, filmed in Melbourne, 10 & 11 April 1980, Australia Council, 1987.

50 Lidoff, *Christina Stead*, p. 183.

51 Cited in Rowley, *Christina Stead*, p. 128.

52 Stead & Blake, *Dearest Munx*, pp. 225 & 268.

53 Stead, *Talking*, p. 316.

54 J. B. Beston, 'An Interview with Christina Stead', *World Literature Written in English*, vol. 15, no. 1, 1976, p. 89.

55 Stead, *Web*, pp. 170 & 392.

56 Chisholm, *National Times*, p. 34.

57 Letter to Edith Anderson, 6 November 1948, National Library of Australia (MS9404-9405).

58 Giuffré, *A Writing Life*, p. 75; Chisholm, *National Times*, p. 34.

59 Giuffré, *A Writing Life*, p. 75.

60 Showalter, *Literature*, p. 84.

61 Cited in ibid., p. 85.

62 Cited in Russ, p. 33.

63 E. Hardwick, *A View of My Own: Essays on Literature and Society*, The Ecco Press, New York, 1962, p. 35.

64 Stead & Blake, *Dearest Munx*, pp. 330–1.

65 P. Johnson, *Creators: From Chaucer to Walt Disney*, Phoenix, London, 2007, p. 121.

66 Drewe, 'Christina Stead', p. 22.

67 Stead, *Talking*, p. 362.

68 ibid., p. 129.

69 Giuffré, *A Writing Life*, p. 74; J. Raskin, 'Christina Stead in Washington Square', *London Magazine*, vol. 9, no. 11, 1970, p. 75; G. Kinross-Smith, 'Christina Stead – Profile', *Westerly*, 1 March 1976, p. 74.

70 Stead, *Web*, pp. 93–4.

71 'Christina Stead: Australian Novelist of Marked Originality', Obituary, *The Times,* 7 April 1983, p. 12.

72 Rowley, *Christina Stead*, p. 204.

73 ibid., p. 285.

74 Notes on *For Love Alone*, National Library of Australia (MS4967/1/2).

75 Lidoff, *Christina Stead*, p. 220.

76 Stead, *Talking*, pp. 88–9.

A Working Writer: Ruth Park

1 R. Park, *A Fence around the Cuckoo*, Penguin, Ringwood, 1992, p. 111.

2 ibid., p. 40.

3   ibid., p. 9.

4   ibid., p. 18.

5   ibid., p. 39.

6   R. Park, *Fishing in the Styx*, Viking, Ringwood, 1993, p. 19.

7   W. Fraser, 'Remembrance of Things Park', Good Weekend, *Sydney Morning Herald*, 5 September 1992, p. 20.

8   R. Park, 'Becoming a Writer', 1988, *Ruth Park: Author*, viewed 4 March 2011, <http://www.ruth-park.com.au/index.htm>.

9   Park, *Fence,* p. 111.

10 ibid., p. 113.

11 ibid., p. 123.

12 ibid., pp. 125–6.

13 ibid., p. 121.

14 ibid., p. 131.

15 ibid., pp. 143–4.

16 ibid., p. 148.

17 ibid., p. 210.

18 ibid., p. 209.

19 Notes for *Fence Around the Cuckoo*. 1989–1990, State Library of NSW (MLMSS 8020, Consignment 5, Box 6).

20 *Fishing in the Styx*: Working journal, begun 27 January 1992, State Library of NSW (MLMSS 8020, Consignment 5, Box 6).

21 Letter to Jocelyn Niland, 7 August 1994, State Library of NSW (MLMSS 8020, Consignment 9, Box 2).

22 Park, *Fence*, p. 217.

23 ibid., pp. 220 & 231.

24 G. Serle, *From Deserts the Prophets Come: The Creative Spirit in Australia 1788–1972*, William Heinemann, Melbourne, 1973, p. 126.

25 Park, *Fishing*, p. 40.

26 Park, *Fence*, p. 246.

27 R. Park & D. Niland, *The Drums Go Bang*, Angus & Robertson, Sydney, 1956, p. 147.

28 ibid., p. 152.

29 ibid., p. 108.

30 Park, *Fishing*, pp. 32 & 39.

31 ibid., p. 78.

32 Cited in ibid., p. 31.

33 Park, *Fence*, p. 278.

34 *Fishing in the Styx*: Working journal.

35 Park, *Fence*, p. 201.

36 Letter to Jill Greaves, December 1994, State Library of NSW (MLMSS 8020, Consignment 9, Box 2).

37 T. O'Connor, 'Ruth Park: A Novel Lifetime', *Courier Mail*, 4 May 1994, p. 9.

38 Fraser, *Sydney Morning Herald*, p. 21.

39 Park, *Fishing*, p. 159.

40 ibid., p. 204.

41 ibid., p. 136.

42 ibid., p. 181.

43 H. De Berg, *Dorothy Hewett interviewed by Hazel De Berg*, sound recording, National Library of Australia, Hazel de Berg collection, 11 March 1973.

44 N. Palmer & V. Palmer, 'It Takes Readers as Well as Writers to Make a Literature', *Australian Writers Speak: Literature and Life in Australia*, Angus & Robertson, Sydney, 1942, p. 94.

45 Park, *Fence*, p. 173.

46 Park & Niland, *Drums*, p. 157.

47 Park, *Fence*, p. 253.

48 Park, *Fishing*, p. 222.

49 ibid., pp. 137–8.

50 ibid., p. 140.

51 Park, *Fence*, pp. 82–3.

52 Letter to Anne Allan Maher, 16 April 1996, State Library of NSW (MLMSS 8020, Consignment 9, Box 2).

53 Letter to Roger Cowell, 30 January 1996, State Library of NSW (MLMSS 8020, Consignment 9, Box 2).

54 Letter to Virginia A. Cullane, 3 June 1996, State Library of NSW (MLMSS 8020, Consignment 9, Box 2).

55 Park, *Fishing*, p. 185.

56 ibid., p. 166.

57 J. Meander, Untitled Column, *Sunday Herald*, 9 October 1949, p. 1.

58 R. Park, 'An Author in Search of a Character', *Sunday Herald*, 19 January 1949, p. 11.

59 Park, *Fishing*, p. 185.

60 ibid., p. 206.

61 ibid., 185.

62 ibid., p. 216.

63 ibid., p. 39.

64 Letter to Rosemary Tribe, Publicity Officer, Penguin Books, 13 January 1994, State Library of NSW (MLMSS 8020, Consignment 9, Box 2).

65 Park, *Fishing*, p. 216.

66 ibid., pp. 77–8.

67 ibid., p. 264.

68 *Fishing in the Styx*: Working journal.

69 Park, *Fishing*, p. 301.

70 Cited in L. Carbines, 'Family the Theme for "Age" Literary Winners', *The Age*, 5 December 1992, p. 19.

71 A. Reimer, 'Hard Times and Paradise', *Sydney Morning Herald*, 5 September 1992, p. 41; Buzo, cited in A. Bennie, 'Literary Friction', The Sydney Magazine, *The Sydney Morning Herald*, 18 June 2003, p. 32.

72 S. Wyndham, 'Undercover', Spectrum, *The Sydney Morning Herald*, 8 August 2009, p. 26.

73 Letter to Jill Greaves, 2 May 1998, State Library of NSW (MLMSS 8020, Consignment 9, Box 2).

74 Park, *Fishing*, p. 284.

75 ibid., p. 301.

Epilogue

1 M. Peake, *Titus Groan* (1946), Vintage, London, 1998, p. 78.

2 R. Park, *Fishing in the Styx*, Viking, Ringwood, 1993, p. 140.

3 C. Stead, *A Web of Friendship: Selected Letters (1928–1973)*, R.G. Geering (ed.), Angus & Robertson, Pymble, 1992, p. 224.

4 H. De Berg, *Dorothy Hewett interviewed by Hazel De Berg*, sound recording, National Library of Australia, Hazel de Berg collection, 11 March 1973.

5 D. Modjeska, *Exiles at Home: Australian Women Writers 1925–1945*, HarperCollins, Sydney, 2001, p. 12.

6 J. Frame, *To the Is-Land: Autobiography 1,* Paladin, London, 1987, p. 44.

7   Oliver Stallybrass, cited in H. Rowley, *Christina Stead: A Biography*, Minerva, Port Melbourne, 1994, pp. 449–50.

8   Stead, *Web*, pp. 74 & 96.

9   J. Digby, *A Woman's Voice: Conversations with Australian Poets*, University of Queensland Press, St Lucia, 1996, p. 229.

10 K. Williamson, 'Unrepentant Spirit', *National Times*, 8–14 Feb 1981, p. 41.

11 G. Kratzmann, *A Steady Storm of Correspondence: Selected Letters of Gwen Harwood 1943–1995*, University of Queensland Press, Brisbane, 2001, p. 64.

12 J. Davidson, *Dorothy Hewett Interviewed by Jim Davidson in Meanjin Collection*, sound recording, 1979, National Library of Australia (ORAL TRC 5217/9).

13 D. Hewett, *Wild Card: An Autobiography 1923–1958*, Penguin, Ringwood, 2001, p. 62.

14 P. Kavanagh, 'An Interview with Dorothy Hewett', *Southerly*, vol. 44, no. 2, 1984, p. 127.

15 K. Veitch, 'A Writer's Life', *ABC Radio 24 Hours*, December 1993, p. 115.

16 Stead, *Web*, p. 348.

Bibliography

Baer, B. L., 'Rereading Christina Stead', Letter to the Editor, Book Review Desk, *The New York Times*, 27 June 2010, p. 5.

Baker, C., *Yacker: Australian Writers Talk About Their Work*, Picador, Sydney, 1986.

Bennett, A., *Our Women*, George H. Doran, New York, 1920.

Bennie, A., 'Literary Friction', The Sydney Magazine, *The Sydney Morning Herald*, 18 June 2003, p. 32.

Beston, J. B., 'An Interview with Christina Stead', *World Literature Written in English*, vol. 15, no. 1, 1976, pp. 87–95.

Boland, E., *Object Lessons: The Life of the Woman and the Poet in Our Times*, Carcanet Press, Manchester, 1995.

Bowen, S., *Drawn from Life: A Memoir* (1941), Pan Macmillan, Sydney, 1999.

Boyd, A. E., *Writing for Immortality: Women and the Emergence of High Literary Culture in America*, Johns Hopkins University Press, Baltimore, 2004.

Carbines, L., 'Family the Theme for "Age" Literary Winners', *The Age*, 5 December 1992, p. 19.

Chisholm, A., 'Stead', *National Times*, 29 March – 4 April 1981, pp. 32–4.

'Christina Stead: Australian Novelist of Marked Originality', Obituary, *The Times*, 7 April 1983, p. 12.

Christina Stead, video, filmed in Melbourne, 10–11 April 1980, Australia Council, 1987.

'Combined recital: pianists and elocutionists', *The Courier Mail*, 7 December 1936, p. 20.

Davidson, J., *Dorothy Hewett interviewed by Jim Davidson in Meanjin Collection*, sound recording, ORAL TRC 5217/9, National Library of Australia, Canberra, 1979.

De Berg, H., *Dorothy Hewett interviewed by Hazel De Berg*, sound recording, Hazel de Berg collection, National Library of Australia, Canberra, 11 March 1973.

Digby, J., *A Woman's Voice: Conversations with Australian Poets*, University of Queensland Press, St Lucia, 1996.

Drewe, R., 'Christina Stead: Interview', in C. Baker (ed.), *Yacker: Australian Writers Talk About Their Work*, Picador, Sydney, 1986.

'Fine Music, Elocution At Prize-giving', *Courier Mail*, 18 May 1940, p. 17.

Frame, J., *To the Is-Land: Autobiography 1*, Paladin, London, 1987.

Fraser, W., 'Remembrance of Things Park', Good Weekend, *Sydney Morning Herald*, 5 September 1992, p. 20.

Giuffré, G., *A Writing Life: Interviews with Australian Women Writers*, Allen & Unwin, Sydney, 1990.

Hardwick, E., *A View of My Own: Essays on Literature and Society*, The Ecco Press, New York, 1962.

Gwen Harwood, video recording, The Writers: Archival Film Series, Australia Council, Sydney, 1987.

Harwood, G., 'Lamplit Presences', *Southerly,* vol. 40, no. 3, 1980, p. 254.

——, 'Memoirs of a Dutiful Librettist', in Robert Sellick (ed.), *Gwen Harwood*, CRNLE Essays & Monographs Series No. 3, Centre for Research in the New Literatures in English, Adelaide, 1987.

——, 'Time Beyond Reason', in Robert Sellick (ed.), *Gwen Harwood*, CRNLE Essays & Monographs Series No. 3, Centre for Research in the New Literatures in English, Adelaide, 1987.

Hewett, D., *Alice in Wormland*, Paper Bark Press, Paddington, NSW, 1987.

——, *Halfway up the Mountain*, Fremantle Arts Centre Press, Fremantle, 2001.

——, *Peninsula*, Fremantle Arts Centre Press, South Fremantle, 1994.

——, *Rapunzel in Suburbia*, Poetry Society of Australia, Sydney, 1975.

——, *The Chapel Perilous, or the Perilous Adventures of Sally Banner* (1972), 3rd edn, Currency Press, Sydney, 1981.

——, *The Toucher,* McPhee Gribble, Ringwood, VIC, 1993.

——, *Wild Card: An Autobiography 1923–1958*, Penguin, Ringwood, 2001.

Hill, B., 'Christina Stead at 80 Says Love Is Her Religion: Interview', *Sydney Morning Herald,* 17 July 1982, p. 33.

Hoddinott, A. (ed.), *Blessed City: Letters to Thomas Riddell 1943*, Collins/Angus & Robertson, Sydney, 1990.

Hoddinott, A. & G. Kratzmann (eds), *Gwen Harwood Collected Poems: 1943–1995*, University of Queensland Press, Brisbane, 2003.

Jarrell, R., 'An Unread Book', introduction, C. Stead, *The Man Who Loved Children*, Harmondsworth, Middlesex, Penguin, 1970.

Johnson, P., *Creators: From Chaucer to Walt Disney*, Phoenix, London, 2007.

Kavanagh, P., 'An Interview with Dorothy Hewett', *Southerly,* vol. 44, no. 2, 1984, pp. 123–42.

Kinross-Smith, G., 'Christina Stead – Profile', *Westerly*, 1 March 1976, pp. 67–75.

Korsmeyer, C., *Gender and Aesthetics: An Introduction*, Routledge, New York, 2004.

Kratzmann, G. (ed.), *A Steady Storm of Correspondence: Selected Letters of Gwen Harwood 1943–1995*, University of Queensland Press, Brisbane, 2001.

Lawrence, D. H., *The Selected Letters of D. H. Lawrence*, Cambridge University Press, Cambridge, 2000.

Lidoff, J., *Christina Stead*, Frederick Ungur Publishing, New York, 1982.

Meander, J., Untitled Column, *Sunday Herald*, 9 October 1949, p. 1.

Modjeska, D., 'Dorothy Hewett Talking with Drusilla Modjeska', in M. Chamberlain (ed.), *Writing Lives: Conversations between Women Writers*, Virago, London, 1988.

——, *Exiles at Home: Australian Women Writers 1925–1945*, HarperCollins, Sydney, 2001.

——, *Stravinsky's Lunch*, Picador, Sydney, 1999.

Moore, N., 'Jill-of-All-Trades', *Overland,* vol. 153, 1998, pp. 34–41.

O'Connor, T., 'Ruth Park: A Novel Lifetime', *Courier Mail*, 4 May 1994, p. 9.

Palmer, N. & V., 'It Takes Readers as Well as Writers to Make a Literature', *Australian Writers Speak: Literature and Life in Australia*, Angus & Robertson, Sydney, 1942.

Park, R., 'An Author in Search of a Character', *Sunday Herald*, 19 January 1949, p. 11.

——, 'Becoming a Writer', 1988, Ruth Park: Author, viewed 4 March 2011, <http://www.ruth-park.com.au/index.htm>.

——, *A Fence around the Cuckoo*, Penguin, Ringwood, 1992.

——, *Fishing in the Styx*, Viking, Ringwood, 1993.

—— & D. Niland, *The Drums Go Bang*, Angus & Robertson, Sydney, 1956.

Peake, M., *Titus Groan* (1946), Vintage, London, 1998.

'Promising young pianist: Mr. Rubinstein impressed', *Courier Mail*, 18 October 1937, p. 17.

Raskin, J., 'Christina Stead in Washington Square', *London Magazine*, vol. 9, no. 11, 1970, pp. 70–7.

Reimer, A., 'Hard Times and Paradise', *Sydney Morning Herald*, 5 September 1992, p. 41.

Rowley, H., *Christina Stead: A Biography*, Minerva, Port Melbourne, 1994.

Russ, J., *How to Suppress Women's Writing*, The Women's Press, London, 1983.

Serle, G., *From Deserts the Prophets Come: The Creative Spirit in Australia 1788–1972*, William Heinemann, Melbourne, 1973.

Showalter, E., *A Literature of Their Own: British Women Novelists from Bronte to Lessing*, Princeton University Press, Princeton, 1977.

'Solo pianist', *The Telegraph* (Brisbane), 1 May 1940, p. 14.

Spires, E., 'The art of poetry No. 27: Elizabeth Bishop', *The Paris Review*, vol. 23, 1981, pp. 57–83.

Stead, C., *A Web of Friendship: Selected Letters (1928–1973)*, R. G. Geering (ed.), Angus & Robertson, Pymble, 1992.

——, *For Love Alone*, Angus & Robertson, London, 1979.

——, *Talking into the Typewriter: Selected Letters (1973–1983)*, R. G. Geering (ed.), Angus & Robertson, Pymble, 1992.

——, *The Man Who Loved Children*, Penguin, Harmondsworth, Middlesex, 1970.

—— & W. J. Blake, *Dearest Munx: The Letters of Christina Stead and William J. Blake*, Margaret Harris (ed.), The Miegunyah Press, Carlton, 2005.

Stewart, H., 'Feminism and Male Chauvinism in the Writings of Christina Stead (1902–1983)', *Hecate*, vol. 29, no. 2, 2003, pp. 113–22.

Tennyson, A., *Poetical Works of Alfred Lord Tennyson*, Macmillan, London, 1908.

Tranter, J., 'Dorothy Hewett interviewed by John Tranter for Radio Helicon (ABC) broadcast 13 May 1987', *Southerly*, vol. 63, no. 2, 2003, pp. 11–19.

Veitch, K., 'A Writer's Life', *ABC Radio 24 Hours*, December 1993, p. 114–18.

Wetherell, R., 'Interview with Christina Stead', *Australian Literary Studies*, vol. 9, no. 4, 1980, pp. 431–48.

Whitehead, A., 'Interview with Christina Stead', *Australian Literary Studies*, vol. 6, no. 3, 1974, pp. 230–48.

Williams, B., 'Interview with Gwen Harwood', *Westerly*, vol. 33, no. 4, 1988, p. 57.

Williams, C., *Christina Stead: A Life of Letters*, McPhee Gribble, Melbourne, 1989.

Williamson, K., 'Unrepentant Spirit', *National Times*, 8–14 February 1981, p. 41.

Woolf, V., *A Room of One's Own/Three Guineas*, Penguin, London, 1993.

Wyndham, S., 'Undercover', Spectrum, *The Sydney Morning Herald*, 8 August 2009, p. 26.

Acknowledgments

In researching and writing this book, I've accumulated many debts. I would like to thank Mrs Alison Hoddinott and Dr Gregory Kratzmann for their generosity in sharing with me not only their own research on Gwen Harwood but also the riches of their personal friendships with her. I am most grateful for the kind hospitality of both, and for the many hours they have suffered my questions and offered their expert views. I would also like to thank the librarians at the Fryer Library, The University of Queensland, for their expertise, endless willingness to go the extra mile, and quiet friendliness when I worked on the Gwen Harwood papers in their collection.

Deborah Niland kindly answered my questions about her mother, Ruth Park, and offered me her insights, for which I am most grateful. Tim Curnow and Rory Niland provided helpful comments on the draft of Chapter 4.

I was most grateful to receive a Varuna Publisher Fellowship for an early version of this manuscript, which enabled me to spend a nourishing week at Varuna in 2012. In addition to the good-comradeship of my fellow writers, I benefitted enormously from the advice I received from Helen Barnes-Bulley, Varuna Writing Consultant. Helen's enthusiasm for the project, and for women writers in general, was catalysing.

Sally Bird's interest in this book, and in the stories of Australian women writers, came at just the right time. I thank her for her faith in this project, her fascination with writers' lives, and her indefatigable efforts on my behalf.

I would also like to thank the judges of the 2017 Dorothy Hewett Award for an Unpublished Manuscript, who highly commended this work. I am so grateful that my work on the revolutionary Dorothy Hewett and her path-breaking contemporaries found a home through an award established in her honour.

On a more personal note, I owe an immeasurable debt to Alice Priest, sister and cheerleader extraordinaire, who joined with me over a number of years in grappling with the question of vocation, bringing her own unique insight to the subject, and who always insisted there were readers out there who would share my peculiar passions. I also want to thank my parents, Jim and Natalie Priest, who have always provided me with safe haven. Finally, I gratefully acknowledge the infinite debt I owe to John Fitzsimmons, who has lived this book with me. His extraordinary knowledge of literature has been an unfailing resource, and his lively engagement through endless hours of conversation helped shape this work. The practical support he has given cannot be measured, but suffice it to say that whenever I have begun a sentence with 'I think I need to travel halfway across the country to read a handful of letters …', he has always responded with a cheerful 'When do we leave?' I couldn't have done it without him.